# Principals of Torts

Law School Notes 2018

FitchLaw, Inc.

**Copyright:**
Copyright 2018 FitchLaw. All rights reserved. No part of this publication may be stored in a retrieval system, transmitted, or reproduced in any way, including but not limited to photocopy, photographs, magnetic, or other record, without the prior agreement and written permission of the publisher.

The author and publisher have made their best efforts to prepare this book. The author and publisher make no representation or warranties of any kind with regards to the completeness or accuracy of the contents herein and accepts no liability of any kind, including but not limited to performance, merchantability, fitness for any particular purpose or any losses or damages of any kind caused or alleged to be caused directly or indirectly from this book.

**Trademarks:**
FitchLaw Inc., has attempted throughout this book to distinguish proprietary trademarks from descriptive terms by following the capitalization style used by the manufacturer. Published by: FitchLaw Inc.

FitchLaw Inc., welcome corrections and comments on its documents. In addition to comments, please send comments on typographical, formatting, or other errors. Simply make a copy of the relevant page, mark the error, and send it to fitchlawupdates@gmail.com. Books and testing materials are available at special quantity discounts to use as premiums and sales promotions, or for corporate training programs, as well as other educational programs.

Printed in the United States of America. No part of this work may be reproduced or transmitted in any form or by any means, electronic, manual, photocopying, recording, or by any information storage and retrieval systems, without prior written permission of the publisher.

ISBN-13: 978-1986237741 (paperback)

# Contents

**1 Overview** — 7
  1.1 Intentional Torts — 7
  1.2 Negligence — 7
  1.3 Strict Liability — 8
  1.4 Damages — 9
  1.5 Vicarious Liability — 9
  1.6 Tort Reform — 9
  1.7 Workers' Compensation — 9
  1.8 Automobile No-Fault — 9
  1.9 Defamation — 9
  1.10 Privacy — 10

**2 Intentional Torts** — 11
  2.1 Intent — 11
    2.1.1 Infancy: *Garratt v. Dailey* — 11
    2.1.2 Insanity: *Williams v. Kearbey* — 12
  2.2 Battery — 12
    2.2.1 Very Small Harms: *Leichtman v. WLW Jacor Commc'ns, Inc.* — 12
    2.2.2 Compliance with Safety Standards: *Bohrmann v. Maine Yankee Atomic Power Co.* — 12
  2.3 Assault — 13
    2.3.1 Liability without Physical Harm: *I de S et Ux v. W de S* — 13
    2.3.2 Forward Looking Verbal Threats: *Castro v. Local 1199, Nat'l Health & Human Servs. Emps. Union* — 13
  2.4 Transferred Intent — 14
    2.4.1 *Alteiri v. Colasso* — 14
  2.5 Mistake Doctrine — 14
  2.6 False Imprisonment — 15
    2.6.1 Implied Threat of Physical Restraint: *Dupler v. Seubert* — 15
  2.7 Malicious Prosecution — 16
    2.7.1 Distinguishing Abuse of Process and Malicious Prosecution: *Maniaci v. Marquette Univ.* — 16
  2.8 Abuse of Process — 17
  2.9 Intentional Infliction of Emotional Distress — 17
    2.9.1 High Threshold for IIED: *Slocum v. Food Fair Stores of Florida, Inc.* — 18
    2.9.2 IIED and Employment: *Rulon-Miller v. International Business Machines Corporation* — 18
    2.9.3 IIED and Sexual Harassment: *Jones v. Clinton* — 18
  2.10 Defenses to Intentional Torts — 18
    2.10.1 Self Defense — 19
    2.10.2 Necessity — 20

- 2.11 Intentional Interference with Contractual and Economic Relations ... 20
  - 2.11.1 *Calbom v. Knudtzon* ... 21
  - 2.11.2 Justified Interference: *Lowell v. Mother's Cake & Cookie Co.* ... 21
  - 2.11.3 Knowledge of a Contract: *Texaco, Inc. v. Pennzoil, Inc.* ... 22
  - 2.11.4 Boycotts: *Environmental Planning & Information Council (EPIC) of Western El Dorado County, Inc. v. Superior Court* ... 22
- 2.12 Wrongful Termination of Employee ... 23
  - 2.12.1 Termination for Protecting the Public Interest: *Foley v. Interactive Data Corp.* ... 23
- 2.13 Tortious Breach of the Covenant of Good Faith and Fair Dealing ... 23
  - 2.13.1 Insurance Company Obligations to Policyholders: *Egan v. Mutual of Omaha Insurance Co.* ... 24
- 2.14 Intentional Misrepresentation ... 24
  - 2.14.1 Authentic Reliance: *Nader v. Allegheny Airlines, Inc.* ... 25

## 3 Negligence  26
- 3.1 Overview ... 26
  - 3.1.1 Foreseeable and Unreasonable: *Pitre v. Employers Liability Assurance Corporation* ... 27
  - 3.1.2 Applying the Hand Formula: *United States Fidelity & Guaranty Co. v. Plovidba* ... 27
- 3.2 Standard of Conduct ... 27
  - 3.2.1 Standard of Care during Emergencies: *Cordas v. Peerless Transp. Co.* ... 27
  - 3.2.2 Mental Illness: *Breunig v. American Family Insurance Company* ... 28
  - 3.2.3 Child Standard and Adult Activity: *Neumann v. Shlansky* ... 28
  - 3.2.4 Professional Standards: *Melville v. Southward* ... 29
  - 3.2.5 Informed Consent: *Cobbs v. Grant* ... 29
- 3.3 Rules of Law and Negligence Per Se ... 30
  - 3.3.1 Rules of Law ... 30
  - 3.3.2 Rule of Law for Baseball Backstops: *Akins v. Glens Falls City School District* ... 30
  - 3.3.3 Negligence Per Se ... 31
  - 3.3.4 Statutory Purpose Doctrine: *Wawanesa Mutual Insurance Co. v. Matlock* ... 31
  - 3.3.5 Interpreting Legislative Intent: *Stachniewicz v. Mar-Cam Corporation* ... 32
  - 3.3.6 Statutory Purpose Doctrine II: *Gorris v. Scott* ... 32
- 3.4 Cause in Fact ... 32
  - 3.4.1 Proving Cause in Fact: *East Texas Theatres, Inc. v. Rutledge* ... 33
  - 3.4.2 Substantial Factor Test: *Anderson v. Minneapolis, St. P. & S. S. M. Ry. Co.* ... 34

|   |   |   |   |
|---|---|---|---|
|   | 3.4.3 | Substantial Factor Test II: *Northington v. Marin* | 34 |
|   | 3.4.4 | Proof of Harm: *Herskovitz v. Group Health Cooperative of Puget Sound* | 34 |
|   | 3.4.5 | Alternate Liability: *Summers v. Tice* | 35 |
|   | 3.4.6 | Market Share Liability: *Sindell v. Abbott Laboratories* | 35 |
|   | 3.4.7 | Toxic Exposure and Uncertain Harm: *Ayers v. Township of Jackson* | 36 |
| 3.5 | Duty and Proximate Cause | | 37 |
|   | 3.5.1 | Common Sense: *Atlantic Coast Line R. Co. v. Daniels* | 37 |
|   | 3.5.2 | *Palsgraf v. The Long Island Railroad Company* | 38 |
|   | 3.5.3 | Directness vs. Foreseeability: *Overseas Tankship (U.K.) Ltd. v. Morts Dock & Engineering Co. (The Wagon Mound) Privy Council* | 38 |
|   | 3.5.4 | Intervening Events: *Thomas v. United States Soccer Fedn.* | 39 |
|   | 3.5.5 | Uncertainty of Foreseeability *Bigbee v. Pacific Telephone and Telegraph Co.* | 39 |
|   | 3.5.6 | The Egg-Shell Plaintiff Rule: *Steinhauser v. Hertz Corporation* | 40 |
| 3.6 | Proof of Negligence: Res Ipsa Loquitur | | 40 |
|   | 3.6.1 | Flying Bodies: *Krebs v. Corrigan* | 41 |
|   | 3.6.2 | *Ybarra v. Spangard* | 42 |
| 3.7 | Limitations on Duty | | 42 |
|   | 3.7.1 | Status and Duty: *L. S. Ayres & Co. v. Hicks* | 43 |
|   | 3.7.2 | Voluntary Interventions: *Miller v. Arnal Corp.* | 43 |
|   | 3.7.3 | Parental Duty: *Wells v. Hickman* | 43 |
|   | 3.7.4 | Therapists and Potential Victims: *Tarasoff v. The Regents of the University of California* | 44 |
|   | 3.7.5 | Police Duty to the Public: *Davidson v. City of Westminster* | 44 |
| 3.8 | Emotional Distress | | 44 |
|   | 3.8.1 | Three Factors for NIED Recovery: *Thing v. La Chusa* | 45 |
|   | 3.8.2 | Fear of Disease from Toxic Exposure: *Potter v. Firestone Tire and Rubber Co.* | 46 |
| 3.9 | Wrongful Death and Survival Actions | | 47 |
|   | 3.9.1 | C.C.P. § 377: Wrongful Death and Survival Actions in California | 47 |
|   | 3.9.2 | Parental Actions for Wrongful Deaths of Children: *Gary v. Schwartz* | 48 |
|   | 3.9.3 | Less Valuable Children: *Selders v. Armentrout* | 48 |
|   | 3.9.4 | Extremely Valuable Children: *Compania Dominicana de Aviacion v. Knapp* | 49 |
| 3.10 | Loss of Consortium, Wrongful Birth, Wrongful Life | | 49 |
|   | 3.10.1 | Loss of Consortium: *Borer v. American Airlines, Inc.* | 50 |
|   | 3.10.2 | Wrongful Life: *Turpin v. Sortini* | 50 |
| 3.11 | Land Occupiers' Duty | | 51 |
|   | 3.11.1 | Merging Trespassers, Licensees, and Invitees: *Rowland v. Christian* | 52 |

|   |   |   |
|---|---|---|
|   | 3.11.2 Duty and Foreseeability: *Ann M. v. Pacific Plaza Shopping Center* | 52 |
|   | 3.11.3 Affirming *Ann M.*: *Wiener v. Southeast Childcare Ctrs., Inc.* | 53 |
| 3.12 | Negligent Misrepresentation and Economic Loss | 53 |
|   | 3.12.1 Negligent Misrepresentation: *Bily v. Arthur Young & Co.* | 54 |
|   | 3.12.2 Economic Loss: *J'Aire Corp. v. Gregory* | 54 |
| 3.13 | Comparative Negligence | 55 |
|   | 3.13.1 Pure Comparative Negligence: *Li v. Yellow Cab Co.* | 56 |
|   | 3.13.2 Assumption of Risk: *Murphy v. Steeplechase Amusement Co.* | 56 |
|   | 3.13.3 Assumption of Risk and Necessity: *Rush v. Commercial Realty Co.* | 57 |
|   | 3.13.4 Thank You Sir, May I Have Another: *Emmette L. Barran, III v. Kappa Alpha Order, Inc.* | 57 |
|   | 3.13.5 Assumption of Risk after *Li*: *Knight v. Jewett* | 57 |
|   | 3.13.6 Veterinarian's Rule: *Priebe v. Nelson* | 58 |
|   | 3.13.7 Primary Assumption of Risk in Non-Contact Sports: *Shin v. Ahn* | 58 |
|   | 3.13.8 Immunity and Government Liability: *Metcalfe v. County of San Joaquin* | 59 |
| 3.14 | Joint and Several Liability | 60 |
|   | 3.14.1 Comparative Indemnity and Cross-Claims: *American Motorcycle Association v. Superior Court* | 60 |
|   | 3.14.2 Proposition 51: Fair Responsibility Act of 1986 | 61 |
| 3.15 | Insurer's Failure to Settle within Policy Limits | 61 |
|   | 3.15.1 *Crisci v. Security Ins. Co.* | 61 |

# 4 Strict Liability 63

| 4.1 | Traditional Strict Liability | 63 |
|---|---|---|
|   | 4.1.1 Abnormally Dangerous Activities: *Siegler v. Kuhlman* | 63 |
|   | 4.1.2 Negligence vs. Strict Liability: *Indiana Harbor Belt Railroad Co. v. American Cyanamid Co.* | 64 |
|   | 4.1.3 Abnormally Dangerous Products vs. Activities: *Kelley v. R.G. Industries, Inc.* | 64 |
|   | 4.1.4 Hazard and Causation: *Foster v. Preston Mill Co.* | 64 |
| 4.2 | Products Liability | 64 |
|   | 4.2.1 Strict Liability for Food and Drugs: *Pillars v. R. J. Reynolds Tobacco Co.* | 66 |
|   | 4.2.2 Origins of Strict Products Liability: *Greenman v. Yuba Power Products, Inc.* | 66 |
|   | 4.2.3 No Privity Required: *Lee v. Crookston Coca-Cola Bottling Co.* | 67 |
|   | 4.2.4 Foreseeable Dangers: *Gray v. Manitowoc Company* | 68 |
|   | 4.2.5 Tobacco-Related Health Problems: *Roysdon v. R.J. Reynolds Tobacco Co.* | 68 |

|   |   |   |
|---|---|---|
| | 4.2.6 Replacing the Consumer Expectations Test: *Barker v. Lull Engineering Co., Inc.* | 68 |
| | 4.2.7 State-of-the-Art Defense: *Beshasda v. Johns-Manville Products Corp.* | 69 |
| | 4.2.8 Federal Preemption: *Riegel v. Medtronic, Inc.* | 70 |
| | 4.2.9 More Federal Preemption: *McKenney v. PurePac Pharmaceutical* | 71 |
| | 4.2.10 Restatement (Third) Approach: *Potter v. Chicago Pneumatic Tool Co.* | 71 |
| | 4.2.11 Economic Damages: *Two Rivers Company v. Curtiss Breeding Service* | 72 |
| | 4.2.12 Comparative Negligence in Strict Products Liability: *Daly v. General Motors Corp.* | 72 |
| | 4.2.13 Applying the *Barker* Test to Component Parts: *Gonzales v. Autoliv* | 73 |

## 5 Damages — 74
5.1 Compensatory Damages — 74
    5.1.1 Loss of Enjoyment and Pain and Suffering: *McDougald v. Garber* — 74
    5.1.2 Collateral Source Rule: *Helfend v. Southern California Rapid Transit District* — 74
5.2 Punitive Damages — 75
    5.2.1 *State Farm Mutual Automobile Ins. Co. v. Campbell* — 75
    5.2.2 Cal. Civ. Code § 3294 — 76

## 6 Vicarious Liability — 77
6.1 Respondeat Superior: *Rodgers v. Kemper Construction Co.* — 77
6.2 Going-and-Coming Rule: *Caldwell v. A.R.B., Inc.* — 77
6.3 Independent Contractors: *Mavrikidis v. Petullo* — 78
6.4 Vicarious Liability for Children: *Wells v. Hickman* — 78

## 7 Tort Reform — 79
7.1 *Fein v. Permanente Medical Group* — 79
7.2 Eisenberg and Sieger, "The Doctor Won't See You Now" — 79
7.3 Treaster and Brinkley, "Behind those Medical Malpractice Rates" — 80
7.4 Colliver, "We Spend Far More, but Our Healthcare is Falling Behind" — 80
7.5 Sack, "Doctors Say 'I'm Sorry' before 'See You in Court'" — 80
7.6 Patient Protection and Affordable Care Act § 6801 — 80

## 8 Workers' Compensation — 81
8.1 Immobility Requirement: *Bletter v. Harcourt, Brace & World, Inc.* — 81
8.2 Off Duty Employees: *Ralphs Grocery v. Workers' Comp. Appeals Bd.* — 81

CONTENTS

|  |  |  |
|---|---|---|
| | 8.3 Special Risk Exception: *Johnson v. Stratlaw, Inc.* | 82 |
| | 8.4 Intentional Torts: *Fermino v. Fedco, Inc.* | 82 |

**9 Automobile No-Fault Insurance** — 84
    9.1 Hager, "No-Fault Drives Again: A Contemporary Primer" — 84

**10 Defamation** — 85
    10.1 Defamatory Assertion of Fact — 85
        10.1.1 *Kaplan v. Newsweek Magazine, Inc.* — 85
        10.1.2 *Kaelin v. Globe Communications, Inc.* — 85
        10.1.3 Defamation in Fiction: *Bindrim v. Mitchell* — 86
    10.2 Libel Versus Slander — 86
        10.2.1 Restatement (Second) — 86
    10.3 Publication — 87
        10.3.1 Publication Requirement for Libel: *Weidman v. Ketcham* — 87
    10.4 Constitutional Culpability Requirement — 88
        10.4.1 Defamation of Public Officals: *New York Times Co. v. Sullivan* — 88
        10.4.2 Defamation of Public Figures: *Gertz v. Robert Welch, Inc.* — 89
        10.4.3 Defamation in Private Affairs: *Dun & Bradstreet, Inc. v. Greenmoss Builders, Inc.* — 89
    10.5 Privileges — 90
        10.5.1 Speech or Debate Clause: *Hutchinson v. Proxmire* — 90
        10.5.2 News Media Privilege: *Brown v. Kelly Broadcasting Co.* — 91

**11 Privacy** — 92
    11.1 Intrusion upon Seclusion — 92
        11.1.1 *Pearson v. Dodd* — 92
        11.1.2 *Dietemann v. Time, Inc.* — 92
    11.2 Appropriation of Name or Likeness — 93
        11.2.1 Newsworthiness: *Neff v. Time, Inc.* — 93
    11.3 Publicity of Private Life — 93
        11.3.1 No Cause of Action if Material is Already Public: *Sipple v. Chronicle Publ'g Co.* — 93
    11.4 False Light — 94
        11.4.1 Distinguishing Common Law and *New York Times* Malice: *Cantrell v. Forest City Publ'g Co.* — 94
    11.5 IIED and Public Figures: *Hustler Magazine v. Falwell* — 95

# § 1 Overview

1. The goal of tort law is to shift the burden of economic loss.

2. Tort law rests on three frameworks:

   (a) Fairness.

   (b) Loss distribution.

   (c) Law and economics.

3. The Supremacy Clause leads to three kinds of **preemption** of federal laws over state laws:

   (a) *Express preemption*: A federal law explicitly or implicitly overrides a state statute.

   (b) *Conflict preemption*: In case of direct conflict, federal law preempts state law.

   (c) *Field preemption*: Congress legislates for an entire field of regulation, leaving no room for states to regulate.

## 1.1 Intentional Torts

1. Definition of intent, infancy, insanity, battery, assault, transferred intent, mistake, false imprisonment, malicious prosecution, abuse of process, intentional infliction of emotional distress, intentional interference with economic and contractual relationships, wrongful termination of employee, tortious breach of the covenant of good faith and fair dealing, intentional misrepresentation.

2. Defenses: self defense, necessity.

## 1.2 Negligence

1. **Overview**.

   (a) Elements of negligence: duty, breach of duty (breach of the standard of care or failure to act as a reasonable person), cause-in-fact, proximate cause, damages.

   (b) Hand formula, foreseeable and unreasonable.

2. **Standard of care**: standard of conduct: emergencies, mental illness, child standard, adult activities, professional standard, informed consent.

3. **Rules of law and negligence per se**: rules of law, negligence per se, statutory purpose doctrine, interpreting legislative intent.

4. **Cause in fact**: cause in fact, foreseeability, proximate case, acting in concert, *Summers v. Tice*/alternative liability test, *Sindell*/market share liability, toxic exposure/uncertain harm.

5. **Duty and proximate cause**: duty, proximate cause, two *Palsgraf* frameworks, two views of proximate cause, intervening superseding events vs. dependent/naturally occurring intervening events, egg-shell plaintiff rule.

6. **Proof of negligence/res ipsa loquitur**: res ipsa loquitur, presumption vs. inference, *Ybarra* rule, Cal Evid. Code § 646.

7. **Limitations on duty**: no duty to act, common law relationships/status, voluntary interventions, parental duty, *Tarasoff*/therapists' duty, police duty.

8. **Emotional distress**: *Amaya*/"zone of danger," *Dillon* (guidelines), *La Chusa* (requirements), toxic exposure,

9. **Wrongful death**: common law vs. modern jurisdictions, named categories of relatives who can recover, damages (pecuniary, pain and suffering, grief), C.C.P. § 377, survival actions, damages in wrongful death vs. damages in survival actions.

10. **Loss of consortium**: loss of consortium, wrongful life, wrongful conception, wrongful birth.

11. **Land occupiers' duty**: common law vs. modern jurisdictions, three legal statuses of visitors (trespassers, invitees, licensees), rejection of visitor's status, *Rowland* factors, child trespassers.

12. **Negligent misrepresentation**: hesitancy on awarding damages for pure economic loss (and *J'Aire*), business relationship requirement, third party recovery.

13. **Comparative negligence**: contributory negligence, modified vs. pure comparative negligence, last clear chance, assumption of risk (primary vs. secondary), *Li*, *Knight*, veterinarians' rule, immunity and government liability, firefighters' rule.

14. **Joint and several liability**: joint liability, several liability, joint and several liability, comparative indemnification (vs. earlier common law rule), contribution vs. indemnification, Prop 51.

15. **Insurer's failure to settle within policy limits.**

## 1.3 Strict Liability

1. **Generally**: policy rationales, abnormally dangerous activities, legislative programs, dangerous products vs. dangerous activities, hazard and causation.

2. **Products liability**: definition, fault vs. loss distribution, comparison to other bases for liability (negligence, express/implied warranty, representation), privity, types of defect (design, manufacturing, warning), issues in defining defect, prescription pharmaceuticals, state-of-the-art defense, Restatement (Third) revisions, recovery for economic damages, comparative negligence, federal preemption, liability for component parts, sophisticated/professional user defense, assumption of risk, tobacco strict liability, *Barker* test/risk–utility.

## 1.4 Damages

1. **Compensatory damages**: loss of enjoyment, pain and suffering, loss of services, collateral source rule.

2. **Punitive damages**: deterrence/retribution, criteria for review (*Gore*), Cal. Civ. Code § 3294.

## 1.5 Vicarious Liability

1. Respondeat superior, going-and-coming rule, independent contractors, children.

## 1.6 Tort Reform

1. MICRA, collateral source rule, subrogation, doctor apologies.

## 1.7 Workers' Compensation

1. Strict liability, no compensatory damages for intangibles, no punitive damages, intentional torts exceptions, bar on negligence claims, going-and-coming rule, special risk exception.

## 1.8 Automobile No-Fault

1. Arguments for and against, pure, partial, choice, neo-partial.

## 1.9 Defamation

1. Libel vs. slander, common law vs. Restatement (Second), harm to reputation, truth defense, libel per se vs. libel per quod, colloquium, right-thinking person, opinion vs. fact, defamation in fiction, proof of special harm in slander and exceptions, New York Times malice, public officials and public figures, absolute privilege, qualified privilege, Speech or Debate Clause, news media privilege.

## 1.10 Privacy

1. Four traditional privacy torts, intrusion upon seclusion, appropriation of name or likeness, publicity of private life, public characterization in a false light, newsworthiness, common law vs. New York Times malice, IIED and public figures.

# § 2 Intentional Torts

## 2.1 Intent

1. Intent requires **desire** or **substantial certainty**.

2. Reckless behavior can sometimes suffice for intent—e.g., IIED, intentional misrepresentation. Substantial certainty is a higher threshold than recklessness.

3. "...the law of torts is not criminal law and does not condemn, but only shifts the burdens of economic loss."[1]

4. Intentional torts are generally excepted from worker's compensation immunity.

5. In most jurisdictions, you can't insure against intentional torts.

6. Restatement (Second) blends purpose and knowledge (i.e., substantial certainty) into one rule. Restatement (Third) proposes separating them into two distinct rules, since limiting liability to "purpose" can have consequences in areas like workplace litigation.

7. Inadvertent results of actions are not intentional. (But, mistakes usually constitute intent—see below. Reasonable mistakes are not allowed except in self defense.)

8. The substantial certainty test significantly expands the use of intentional torts in workplace and environmental litigation.

9. A few jurisdictions have rejected the substantial certainty rule.[2]

### 2.1.1 Infancy: *Garratt v. Dailey*

Infancy is not a defense to intentional torts.

1. A five year old moved a chair from the place where the plaintiff was about to sit. The plaintiff fell and fractured her hip.

2. The court held that the plaintiff's battery claim required proof that the defendant intended to cause contact that was not consensual or otherwise privileged. Restatement (Second) indicates that intent exists if the actor is **substantially certain** that the harmful contact **will** (not might) occur.

3. The court found that it was unclear whether the defendant was substantially certain that the result would occur. Remanded to the trial court for clarification.

---

[1] *Understanding Torts*, p. 6.
[2] Casebook p. 6.

### 2.1.2 Insanity: *Williams v. Kearbey*

Insanity is not a defense to intentional torts.

1. Kearbey, a minor, shot up a school and claimed insanity.

2. The court held that Kearbey intended to commit the action, even if his motivation was irrational, and was therefore liable.

## 2.2 Battery

1. Battery requires **intent to cause harmful or offensive contact** and that harmful or offensive contact directly or indirectly results.

    (a) "Unpermitted" touching can be enough—see *White v. University of Idaho*, where a piano teacher touched a student's back and caused significant injury.

    (b) Any touching in anger can also be enough.

2. The proposed Third Restatement would limit intent liability based on substantial certainty to small, localized groups of people. So, for instance, tobacco companies would not be liable for second-hand smoke damages.

### 2.2.1 Very Small Harms: *Leichtman v. WLW Jacor Commc'ns, Inc.*

Minuscule contact can constitute battery, though recovery for damages will likely be minimal.

1. A cigar smoker and talkshow host employed by WLW Jacor blew smoke in the face of Leichtman, an anti-smoking advocate.

2. The court found that "[n]o matter how trivial the incident, a battery is actionable..."[3] But it rejected the "smoker's battery," which imposes liability if there is substantial certainty that second-hand smoke will touch a nonsmoker.[4]

### 2.2.2 Compliance with Safety Standards: *Bohrmann v. Maine Yankee Atomic Power Co.*

Compliance with safety standards has no bearing on liability for intentional torts.

1. The plaintiffs, several University of Southern Maine students, took a tour of a nuclear power plant. They alleged the power company knew a flushing procedure would release radioactive gases during the tour and that tour

---

[3]Casebook p. 11.
[4]Casebook p. 16 n. 6.

# 2 INTENTIONAL TORTS

guides knowingly took students through plumes of unfiltered radioactive gases. They also allege the company falsely told them they had not been exposed to "bad" radiation.

2. The court held that compliance with federal safety standards did not affect the power company's liability for its intentional acts.

## 2.3 Assault

1. Assault is the threat or use of force on another that causes that person to have a **reasonable apprehension of imminent harmful or offensive contact**.

2. Restatement (Second) does not require apprehension to be "reasonable," but most courts do.

3. **Assault in torts is different than assault in criminal law.** The criminal law definition requires an attempt to inflict harmful or offensive contact, but it does not require the victim's perception.[5]

### 2.3.1 Liability without Physical Harm: *I de S et Ux v. W de S*

Damages be awarded if physical harm did not occur.

1. The Defendant tried to buy wine from the plaintiff. He beat on the door with a hatchet. When the plaintiff's wife asked him to stop, he tried to hit her with the hatchet but did not hit her.

2. The court ruled that the plaintiff was entitled to damages even though no physical harm was done.

### 2.3.2 Forward Looking Verbal Threats: *Castro v. Local 1199, Nat'l Health & Human Servs. Emps. Union*

To constitute assault, verbal threats must accompany "circumstances inducing a reasonable apprehension of bodily harm."

1. Plaintiff had asthma, which prevented her from working in extremely hot or cold situations. After a disability leave, she attended a meeting where she didn't receive her usual assignment. She asked what was going on, and Frankel (another employee) replied, "if I was you, I would take whatever they give me, because you could lose more than your job." When asked he was threatening her life, Frankel said, "Take it any way you want."[6]

---

[5]Casebook p. 21.
[6]Casebook p. 18.

## 2 INTENTIONAL TORTS

2. The court held that verbal threats, without "circumstances inducing a reasonable apprehension of bodily harm," do not constitute an assault. Here, the threat was "forward-looking" and did not suggest imminent harm.[7] The court granted the defendant's motion for summary judgment.

3. Prior behavior can furnish the necessary attendant circumstances. See *Campbell v. Kansas State University*, where a university head said "he felt like hitting his assisstant on the buttocks, after he had already slapped her on the buttocks," which the court held to be assault.[8]

### 2.4 Transferred Intent

1. Generally, **intent towards anyone for any intentional tort is intent towards anyone else for any other tort**.

2. Historically, transferred intent means that intent to commit any of the five traditional torts (battery, assault, false imprisonment, trespass to land, trespass to chattel—because these are torts where you would file a writ of trespass in old English contexts) can constitute the necessary intent to commit any of the other five.

3. Transferred intent is a legal fiction.

4. Restatement (Second) only incorporates transferred intent for assault and battery.

#### 2.4.1 *Alteiri v. Colasso*

The intended target doesn't matter as long as the defendant intended to commit the act.

1. Colasso threw a rock that hit Alteiri in the eye, but he intended to scare somebody else. He did not intend to hit anyone, and he did not throw the rock recklessly.

2. The court held that there was no error in the jury's verdict for willful battery.

### 2.5 Mistake Doctrine

1. **Mistake is not a defense to intentional torts**, even if the mistake was reasonable.

2. *Ranson v. Kittner*: the defendant was liable for shooting a dog, even though he believed it was a wolf.

3. However, reasonable mistakes are usually permitted in self defense.

---

[7] Casebook p. 19.
[8] Casebook p. 20.

## 2.6 False Imprisonment

1. False imprisonment is **intentional, unlawful, and unconsented restraint**.

2. According to the Restatement (Second), confinement may be caused by:

    (a) Physical barriers.

    (b) Force or threat of immediate force.

    (c) Omissions where there is a duty to act.

    (d) False arrest.

3. Victim must be confined in a bounded area (e.g., if movement is allowed in any direction, even if it's not the desired direction, false imprisonment did not occur).

4. The victim must usually be conscious of confinement, but not always (e.g., infant abduction).

5. False imprisonment usually does not recognize highly coercive but non-physical threats (e.g., economic retaliation).

6. Lawful restraint does not constitute false imprisonment

7. *Shopkeeper's privilege*: Shopkeepers can detain suspected shoplifters.

8. "[A] form of false imprisonment whereby the improper assertion of legal authority can unlawfully restrain a victim."[9]

### 2.6.1 Implied Threat of Physical Restraint: *Dupler v. Seubert*

1. Dupler was fired from her job. Her superiors, including Seubert, kept her against her will in a 1.5-hour meeting. Dupler claimed that Seubert and the other defendant screamed and shouted at her.

2. The trial jury found Seubert liable for false imprisonment and awarded damages of $7,500. The trial judge offered a remittitur of $500, and Seubert appealed. The Supreme Court of Wisconsin affirmed the order, holding that false imprisonment occurred when Dupler was held against her will after her hours of employment had ended at 5 PM (in contrast to *Weiler v. Herzfeld-Phillipson*, where the imprisonment occurred during work hours).

---

[9]Casebook p. 38 n. 1.

## 2.7 Malicious Prosecution

1. Restatement (Second) requires:

    (a) Initiation of proceedings **without probable cause and for a purpose other than bringing the offender to justice**.

    (b) **Termination of the proceedings in favor of the accused**—so, a defendant who is sued and loses can't claim malicious prosecution (i.e., the defendant must have been exonerated to have a cause of action for malicious prosecution).[10]

2. Anti-SLAPP statutes also help prevent against frivolous litigation.

3. Some jurisdictions recognize malicious prosecution only in criminal contexts, with the parallel civil tort "wrongful institution of civil proceedings."[11]

4. The "American Rule" dictates that the loser in a suit doesn't have to pay the winner's legal fees (in contrast to the "British Rule").

### 2.7.1 Distinguishing Abuse of Process and Malicious Prosecution: *Maniaci v. Marquette Univ.*

There can be no malicious prosecution without malice.

1. Saralee Maniaci, a student at Marquette University, decided to leave the school. She got her father's permission.

2. School administrators tried to persuade her not to leave. When they were unsuccessful, they requested that the Milwaukee police bring papers for temporary emergency detention in a mental hospital for people considered "irresponsible and dangerous." The school physician, the Dean of Women, and a registered nurse signed the application for temporary custody. Maniaci was held for a night until her father demanded her release.

3. She and her father filed suit on multiple charges, all of which were dismissed except false imprisonment. The jury assessed compensatory and punitive damages, which the court reduced on motions after the verdict.

4. On appeal, the defendants argued that the only legitimate cause of action was **malicious prosecution**, that the evidence was insufficient to prove malicious prosecution, and that the damages were excessive.

5. The appellate court agreed that there was no cause of action for false imprisonment because the restraint was "lawful." It did not find a cause of action for malicious prosecution because there was no malice since the defendants "had a genuine concern for the plaintiff's welfare."

---

[10] Understanding Torts p. 48.
[11] Casebook p. 39 n. 2.

6. However, the court found support—"skeletally at least"—for a cause of action for abuse of process. The defendants did not have serious concerns about Maniaci's mental health. Rather, their purpose was to restrain her until her parents had been notified of her decision to leave school, and had either given their permission or directed Saralee to stay in school.

7. Reversed.

## 2.8 Abuse of Process

1. Abuse of process is the **misuse of legal process for an ulterior purpose**.

2. Unlike malicious prosecution, it does not require termination of the legal process in favor of the one bringing the complaint (or even termination at all).

3. See *Maniaci*, above.

## 2.9 Intentional Infliction of Emotional Distress

1. "Intentional infliction of emotional distress **occurs when the defendant, through extreme and outrageous conduct, intentionally or recklessly causes the victim severe emotional distress.**"[12]

2. It can overlap with other torts—e.g., wrongful termination, sexual/racial harassment.

3. It is not a historic tort, but a product of the 20th century. The torts (above) all have rigid factors. Courts invented intentional infliction to get around these restrictions.

4. There is no need to prove physical injury.

5. Most states require a showing from the defendant of outrageous behavior beyond all reasonable bounds of decency.

6. The relationship between the plaintiff and defendant can impact the court's characterization of the conduct as extreme or outrageous.

7. The plaintiff's sensitivity usually isn't enough—e.g., *Nickerson v. Hodges*, where a woman believed her dead relatives had buried a pot of gold in her backyard. The defendants buried a pot of dirt, which she opened at the bank, expecting gold. The court found that the joke caused her extreme distress.

---

[12]Casebook p. 44 n. 1.

### 2.9.1 High Threshold for IIED: *Slocum v. Food Fair Stores of Florida, Inc.*

There is a high threshold for behavior that constitutes gross recklessness or intent to cause severe distress.

1. A shopper in a store asked the price of an item. An employee replied, "if you want to know the price, you'll have to find out the best way you can...you stink to me." She had a heart attack and sued for intentional infliction of emotional distress.

2. The appellate court denied the claim, reasoning that the language did not constitute "gross recklessness," nor was it intended to cause "severe emotional distress."

3. Would racial identities have affected the court's holding?

4. Levy thinks *Slocum* is wrong—the appellate court should have taken the jury's verdict into account.

### 2.9.2 IIED and Employment: *Rulon-Miller v. International Business Machines Corporation*

Restricting an employee's rights can constitute IIED.

1. The plaintiff, a longtime IBM employee carried on a relationship with an employee at a rival office products firm, QYX. Her managers at first indicated they did not think the relationship constituted a conflict of interest—"I don't have any problem with that." But then her manager told her to end the relationship or lose her job, giving her "a couple of days to a week" to think about it. The next day, he said "he had made up her mind for her" and dismissed her.

2. The court held that the manager "intended to emphasize that she was powerless to to do anything to assert her rights," affirming the judgment for intentional infliction of emotional distress.

### 2.9.3 IIED and Sexual Harassment: *Jones v. Clinton*

Sexual harassment does not necessarily indicate IIED.

1. Paula Jones claimed Bill Clinton's "actual exposure of an intimate private body part" constituted extreme and outrageous conduct.

2. The court found no evidence that the incident caused any significant lasting emotional distress and rejected the claim in a summary judgment.

## 2.10 Defenses to Intentional Torts

1. The burden of proof is on the defendant (i.e., the one raising the defense).

## 2 INTENTIONAL TORTS

### 2.10.1 Self Defense

1. Force intended to inflict death or serious injury must be necessary and is only reasonable in response to the **immediate threat of serious bodily injury or death**.

2. The Restatement of Torts also requires retreat if safely possible (except from the victim's own dwelling) before the victim can respond with force intended to inflict serious bodily injury or death. Most courts disagree.[13]

3. If the threat is not immediate, self-defense is not valid. There is dispute about spousal abuse cases, however—should the smaller spouse be required to wait until the physical threat is immediate before asserting the right to self-defense?

4. The immediate threat requirement is controversial in spousal abuse cases.

5. Reasonable mistakes in perceiving threats can be valid bases for self defense.

6. There is a limited right to self defense against excessive police force.

7. Should good samaritans be encouraged to intervene? The Second Restatement allows bystanders to assert self defense if they reasonably believe that the third party has a privilege of self defense and that intervention is necessary to protect him. The traditional rule, however, only allows intervention when the third party is actually privileged. The Second Restatement would allow reasonable mistakes, but the common law rule does not.

8. Self defense includes protection of members of the defendant's family and workplace.

9. Reasonable force is allowed to protect property. Force intended to inflict death or serious bodily injury (e.g., spring guns in barns) is never allowed.

10. Defense of others generally does not apply to unborn fetuses.

11. Private citizens can use reasonable force to arrest others who committed felonies or when the felony occurred and the citizen reasonably believes the person arrested is guilty. Private citizens can also arrest others they witness committing misdemeanors.

### *Drabek v. Sabley*

1. Ten-year-old Drabek and friends were throwing snowballs at passing cars. One driver, Sabley, stopped, caught Drabek, took him by the arm to his car, and drove him back to the village of Williams Bay. He turned Drabek over to the police. Drabek was with Sabley for a total of 15-20 minutes.

---
[13] Casebook p. 64.

2. The court held that Sabley was justified in preventing the commission of a crime, and so it was reasonable to admonish Drabek and march him home. But it was not reasonable to detain him and take him to the police station, so Sabley was liable for false imprisonment and nominal battery.

3. Remanded to determine compensatory (but not punitive) damages.

### 2.10.2 Necessity

1. "**Private necessity** is a privilege which allows the defendant to interfere with the property interests of an innocent party in an effort to avoid a greater injury. The privilege is incomplete since the actor must still compensate the victim for the property."[14]

2. The defendant must have **reasonably perceived** the need to appropriate the victim's property to avoid a greater damage to property or life.

3. "The defense of **public necessity** allows the appropriation of property to avoid a greater harm to the public"[15]—e.g., destroying a building to prevent a fire from spreading to the rest of the city. Compensation to the property owner is not required.

*Vincent v. Lake Erie Transp. Co.*

1. The defendant was moored at the plaintiff's dock to unload goods when a severe storm struck. He kept his boat secured (and repeatedly replaced damaged or broken lines) to the dock throughout the storm, causing $500 in damages to the dock.

2. The court held that private necessity meant the defendant was justified in using another's property due to the extreme circumstances but was responsible for the damages he incurred.

## 2.11 Intentional Interference with Contractual and Economic Relations

1. Economic torts: we want competition, but not too much.

2. Contractual interference torts are rooted in anti-labor motivations.

3. According to the Second Restatement, the elements of these two torts are:

    (a) A valid contract or economic expectancy.

    (b) Defendant's knowledge of the contract or economic expectancy.

    (c) Defendant's intent to interfere.

---

[14]Casebook pp. 69–70.
[15]Casebook p. 71.

## 2 INTENTIONAL TORTS

(d) Interference.

(e) Damage to the plaintiff.[16]

4. The plaintiff bears the burden of proof. The plaintiff must show that the interference was not justified.

5. Many courts recognize various justifications:

    (a) Fair competition or proper protection of one's own financial interest (as long as the contract is freely terminable at will).

    (b) Protecting the welfare of another for whom one is responsible.

    (c) Providing truthful or honest information if requested.

    (d) Assertion of a bona fide property right (e.g., preventing a thief from selling your car).

    (e) Interfering with an agreement that is illegal or against public policy.

6. Not all courts treat these as distinct torts, though California does.

7. For non-legal reasons (e.g., public relations), these torts are rarely brought (do you really want to sue several people for leaving your firm?).

8.

### 2.11.1 *Calbom v. Knudtzon*

1. Mr. Henderson died and left Mrs. Henderson to execute his estate. Harry Calbom, a lawyer, had been hired to help sort out the legal issues. Mrs. Henderson's accountant, Mr. Knudtzon, told Mrs. Henderson that Calbom was unsatisfactory and provided a list of other attorneys. Mrs. Henderson found another attorney.

2. Calbom sued for intentional interference with his employment contract. The court held that an attorney-client relationship existed, which Calbom had every right to expect would continue. It found that the "defendants' interference was malicious, intentional, and without justification," affirming the judgment for Calbom.

    (a) Levy: this case is wrong. Knudtzon gave multiple suggestions for other attorneys, and there is no evidence of favoritism or kickbacks.

### 2.11.2 Justified Interference: *Lowell v. Mother's Cake & Cookie Co.*

"...intentional interference with prospective economic advantage constitutes actionable wrong *if* it results in damages to the plaintiff, and the defendant's conduct is not excused by a legally recognized privilege or justification."[17]

---

[16] Casebook p. 82 n. 1.
[17] Casebook p. 87.

1. The owner of Lowell Freight Lines had a longstanding oral contract with Mother's. He planned to sell the company. Mother's told prospective purchasers that it would terminate the delivery contract if Lowell sold the company. Lowell sold the company for $17,400 instead of the alleged true market value of $200,000.

2. The trial court granted Mother's demurrer.

3. The appellate court reversed, holding that Lowell stated a cause of action for tortious interference with prospective business advantage and that Mother's justification failed to appear on the face of the complaint.

### 2.11.3 Knowledge of a Contract: *Texaco, Inc. v. Pennzoil, Inc.*

Knowledge of a contract (even if only an oral contract) and intent to cause its breach are sufficient to constitute intentional interference.

1. Pennzoil was negotiating an oral contract with Getty in which Pennzoil would purchase Getty stock. The trial jury found that the contract had been established and that Texaco intentionally interfered with the agreement. It awarded $7.53 billion in compensatory damages and $3 billion in punitive damages.

2. On appeal, the issues were (1) whether there was a binding contract between Getty and Pennzoil and (2) whether Texaco knowingly induced a breach of the contract.

3. The appellate court found that the contract was valid and enforceable.

4. The appellate court also found that knew of the agreement and actively induced its breach.

5. The appellate court affirmed but reduced the punitive damage award.

### 2.11.4 Boycotts: *Environmental Planning & Information Council (EPIC) of Western El Dorado County, Inc. v. Superior Court*

Political expression is protected from intentional interference actions if the defendant provides only truthful information.

1. Detmold, a newspaper, sued EPIC for criticizing Detmold's editorial policies on environmental issued, urging its readers to boycott business that advertised in Detmold's paper. The state court denied EPIC's motion for summary judgment.

2. On appeal, the California Supreme Court held that EPIC was advocating a political boycott and was thus protected. Reversed (granting summary judgment for EPIC.)

## 2.12 Wrongful Termination of Employee

1. An employer can be liable for wrongful termination if the termination contradicts significant public policy.

2. Unless otherwise indicated explicitly or implicitly, the employment contract is at-will.

3. Traditionally, a breach of an employment contract would only lead to contract damages, which are smaller than tort damages. Leading plaintiff's lawyers developed the tort of wrongful discharge, which holds the employer liable for emotional distress and punitive damages (in addition to breach-of-contract damages).

4. A cause of action exists only if the firing breaches constitutional or statutory public policy.

### 2.12.1 Termination for Protecting the Public Interest: *Foley v. Interactive Data Corp.*

Employees can recover damages if their firing resulted from actions they took to protect the public interest. However, it is not enough to merely protect the employer's private interests.

1. A well-regarded employee, Foley, became concerned when he learned that the person hired to be a new Vice President was under FBI investigation for embezzlement from Bank of America, his previous employer. Foley was fired within a few days

2. The court found that there was no wrongful termination because Foley's disclosure benefited only the private interests of his employer, not the public.

## 2.13 Tortious Breach of the Covenant of Good Faith and Fair Dealing

1. **Every contract imposes a duty of good faith and fair dealing**. Some courts hold that a breach of this covenant constitutes a tort, allowing tort damages (e.g., punitive damages and compensation for mental distress) as well as breach-of-contract remedies.

2. CA was the first state to develop the tort. It arose in the context of bad faith breaches of insurance contexts and then later extended to other contexts. But, after 1986 political swing in the California courts, the rule became that actions for bad faith are only allowed in insurance cases.

3. There are two types of insurance: first party (which bets on whether an event will happen—disability, life, etc.) and third party (which addresses incidents involving third parties—liability, homeowners, auto, etc.).

## 2 INTENTIONAL TORTS

4. Many courts have limited this tort to insurance contexts. However, as many as 16 of the 36 states that recognize the tort have applied it to non-insurance contexts.[18]

### 2.13.1 Insurance Company Obligations to Policyholders: *Egan v. Mutual of Omaha Insurance Co.*

1. Egan purchased a disability insurance policy from Omaha Insurance. When the plaintiff became disabled, the insurance company withheld payments, calling the plaintiff a "fraud."

2. The court found that Omaha wrongly and maliciously withheld payment. It held that an insurer "cannot reasonably and in good faith deny payments to its insured without thoroughly investigating the foundation for its denial." The court found for the plaintiff (but deemed the punitive damages of $5 million to be excessive).

## 2.14 Intentional Misrepresentation

1. Restatement (Second): "One who fraudulently makes a [material] misrepresentation of fact, opinion, intention or law for the purpose of inducing another to act or to refrain from action in reliance upon it, is subject to liability to the other in deceit for pecuniary loss caused to him by his justifiable reliance upon the misrepresentation."[19]

2. **Misrepresentation must be intentional or reckless.** It usually has to be a statement of fact, not opinion, except in the case of a fiduciary.

3. Cal. Civ. Code § 1710 defines actionable deceit.[20]

4. Courts have traditionally **not included** broken promises within this tort (though they may constitute breach of contract). However, some courts and the Restatement (Second) have begun to distinguish between promises that are lies (which are tortious) and sincere promises.[21]

5. Failure to disclose can constitute concealment.

---

[18]Casebook p. 115.
[19]Casebook p. 121.
[20]A deceit, within the meaning of the last section, is either:

(a) The suggestion, as a fact, of that which is not true, by one who does not believe it to be true;

(b) The assertion, as a fact, of that which is not true, by one who has no reasonable ground for believing it to be true;

(c) The suppression of a fact, by one who is bound to disclose it, or who gives information of other facts which are likely to mislead for want of communication of that fact; or,

(d) A promise, made without any intention of performing it.

[21]Casebook p. 124.

### 2.14.1 Authentic Reliance: *Nader v. Allegheny Airlines, Inc.*

To successfully recover, a plaintiff must have authentically relied on the misrepresentation.

1. Allegheny Airlines bumped Nader from a flight, causing him to miss a speaking engagement. The airline intentionally overbooked the flight but told all passengers that they had "confirmed reservations."

2. Allegheny argued that "confirmed" was reasonable language because the probability of being bumped was very low.

3. The trial court held that the airline's nondisclosure was misleading. It awarded $10 in compensatory damages to Nader and $15,000 in punitive damages.

4. The appellate court reversed, arguing that Nader's reliance was not justifiable because he had been bumped many times before and knew about the airline's policy. He had not authentically relied on the misrepresentation.

## § 3  Negligence

### 3.1  Overview

"To prevail on an action in negligence, plaintiffs must show that defendants owed them a legal duty, that they breached the duty, and that the breach was a proximate or legal cause of their injuries."[22]

1. Negligence is "the failure to exercise the standard of care that a **reasonably prudent [careful] person** would have exercised in a similar situation."[23]

2. Negligence requires proof that the defendant acted unreasonably.

3. The standard of care is objective.

4. Negligence has **five factors**:

    (a) Duty.

    (b) Breach of duty.

    　　i. Breach of the standard of care.

    　　ii. Failure to act as a reasonably careful person would under the circumstances.

    (c) Cause-in-fact.

    (d) Proximate cause.

    (e) Damages.

5. Tort law generally doesn't lower the standard of care for people who are unable to meet it.

6. The **Hand Formula** is Judge Learned Hand's test for determining negligence. It works best in scenarios where the actor takes a calculated risk (e.g., business decisions). It is less useful in cases where the actor was simply not paying attention.

    (a) B = Burden of precautions necessary to prevent an accident.

    (b) P = Probability that an accident will occur.

    (c) L = Magnitude of the loss if the accident occurs.

    (d) **Negligence exists if B<PL**—i.e., if the burden of precautions is less than the harm multiplied by the probability of occurrence.

7. Prosser: compare the utility of the risk with the gravity of the loss.

---

[22] *Wiener v. Southcoast Childcare Ctrs., Inc.*, 32 Cal. 4th 1138 (2004) (below).
[23] Black's Law.

## 3 NEGLIGENCE

### 3.1.1 Foreseeable and Unreasonable: *Pitre v. Employers Liability Assurance Corporation*

**Negligence occurs only if the danger is both foreseeable and unreasonable.**

1. The plaintiffs' son died when a patron at a carnival game was winding up a pitch and hit him in the head.

2. The trial court found in favor of the plaintiffs.

3. The appellate court held that the key factor was how a "reasonably prudent individual" would have acted or what precautions he would have taken under similar circumstances. The court held that the danger was foreseeable but not unreasonable, and therefore there was no negligence.

### 3.1.2 Applying the Hand Formula: *United States Fidelity & Guaranty Co. v. Plovidba*

If the probability of the accident occurring is very small, the court will likely not find the defendant to be negligent.

1. Inside a dark room, the hatch to a cargo hold on a ship was left open. A longshoreman fell through it and died.

2. The trial court found for the defendant.

3. Richard Posner, writing for the Seventh Circuit, applied the Hand Formula, reasoning that B was relatively small (it would have been easy to close the hatch or leave a light turned on) and L was high (the victim died). P, however, was very small. There was no reason for the longshoreman to enter the hold. In fact, he was probably there to steal liquor, and the evidence suggests he knew the hatch was open and tried to skirt around it. The shipowner was therefore not negligent.

## 3.2 Standard of Conduct

### 3.2.1 Standard of Care during Emergencies: *Cordas v. Peerless Transp. Co.*

In emergencies, people are held to a lower standard of care. Or, behavior that would otherwise be unreasonable is allowed in emergencies.

1. A man was mugged at gunpoint by two other men in New York City. He chased after them. One of the muggers jumped into a taxi, held the driver at gunpoint, and told him to drive. While the cab was in motion, the driver jumped out, and a few seconds later, so did the hijacker. The cab crashed into a sidewalk and injured the defendants.

2. The trial court held that the driver was not negligent because he acted as a reasonable person would act under similar circumstances.

3. Courts are divided on the question of whether juries should receive special instructions regarding negligence claims in emergency circumstances. On the one hand, it is redundant to reiterate that a defendant must be held to the standard of what a reasonable person would do in a similar emergency situation. Others claim it helps clarify the standard.

4. **Conditional privilege**: choose the lesser of two harms.

### 3.2.2 Mental Illness: *Breunig v. American Family Insurance Company*

The majority view, including in California, holds that insanity is not a defense to negligence.

1. A schizophrenic woman had a psychotic episode while driving her car. The question was whether she had foreknowledge of her susceptibility to such attacks.

2. The general rule is that **insanity or another mental deficiency does not limit liability for negligence**. The court here noted that the rule may be too harsh because it excludes the insanity defense when a driver is suddenly overcome without warning.

3. The Supreme Court agreed with the lower courts that the defendant did have the necessary foreknowledge, and held for the plaintiff.

4. There are **two frameworks for assessing liability from the sudden onset of mental illness**:

    (a) Fairness: it's not fair to punish someone who could not have avoided having a seizure.

    (b) Loss distribution: if someone has to bear the cost of repairing the harm, it should be the perpetrator, not the victim.

5. One view: insanity constitutes a defense if there was no warning.

6. Majority view (including CA): insanity does not create any defense as to compensatory damages. Physical ailments, however, are taken into account.

### 3.2.3 Child Standard and Adult Activity: *Neumann v. Shlansky*

Children are held to the standard of a **reasonable person of like age, intelligence, and experience under the circumstances** unless they are engaging in an adult (or inherently dangerous activity).

# 3  NEGLIGENCE

1. An eleven-year-old hit a golf ball that struck the defendant in the knee, causing serious injury.

2. Generally, children are held to the standard of a **reasonable person of like age, intelligence, and experience under the circumstances.** In this case, however, the child was engaging in an "adult activity," and therefore the court held him to the adult reasonable person standard.

3. Some states are moving from "adult activity" to "inherently dangerous activity."

### 3.2.4  Professional Standards: *Melville v. Southward*

In many professions (e.g., medicine, engineering, accounting, and a few others) the "competent professional" standard replaces the "reasonable person" standard.

1. The defendant, a podiatrist, operated on the plaintiff's foot. The plaintiff sued for malpractice, and introduced the testimony of an orthopedist, who questioned the necessity and sanitation of the operation.

2. The question before the court was whether the orthopedist, a practitioner from a different school of medicine, should have been allowed to testify about the standard of care in podiatry.

3. The trial court allowed the orthopedist to testify.

4. The Supreme Court of Colorado here agreed with the appellate court that the testimony should not have been allowed because it was "nothing more than an expression of opinion that that the general practice of podiatry did not meet the standard of care observed by an orthopedic surgeon." Reversed.

5. There is disagreement about whether doctors in rural areas should be held to different standards than urban doctors.

6. Medical specialists in the same geographic region are often reluctant to testify against each other—a "conspiracy of silence."

7. In a limited range of cases, a jury of laypeople can determine whether a practice met an acceptable standard of care.

### 3.2.5  Informed Consent: *Cobbs v. Grant*

Doctors are required to obtain **informed consent** from patients. Failure to obtain informed consent can expose a physician to negligence liability.

1. The plaintiff here sued a doctor who operated on a stomach ulcer but did not discuss the surgery's inherent risks. Complications developed, another operation was required, more complications developed, and so on.

2. The plaintiff argued that (1) the doctor acted negligently in the performance of the surgery (on which the jury found in favor of the plaintiff) and (2) that the doctor failed to obtain informed consent.

3. The Supreme Court of California here noted that courts are divided as to whether this type of tort should be deemed a **battery or negligence**. The court aligned itself with a "majority trend" that advocates reserving battery for cases where a doctor performs an operation without the patient's consent.

4. Generally, physicians are required to tell patients about major risks (but not every minor risk) and obtain the patient's consent.

5. In this case, the court found that there was not enough evidence to show that the doctor acted negligently. Reversed.

6. Failure to obtain informed consent can expose a physician to negligence liability. Unless the physician misrepresents the entire procedure, most courts will not characterize the behavior as intentional battery.

## 3.3 Rules of Law and Negligence Per Se

### 3.3.1 Rules of Law

1. Juries are typically responsible for determining what constitutes reasonable conduct under the circumstances. Judges, however, will sometimes establish a **rule of law** for what constitutes negligent conduct under particular circumstances.

2. For instance, in *Baltimore & Ohio R.R.*, Justice Holmes established a rule requiring drivers to get out of their cars and examine railroad crossings ("stop, look, and listen").

3. Most courts do not use this approach because it's premised on repetition of fact patterns. Fact patterns are rarely identical. Judges may also not make the best rules (e.g., Holmes).

### 3.3.2 Rule of Law for Baseball Backstops: *Akins v. Glens Falls City School District*

1. A foul ball injured a spectator at a baseball game. She sued the ballpark's owners, the local school district, for negligence.

2. The trial court held in favor of the plaintiff.

3. The appellate court reversed, finding that the school district had not acted negligently, and establishing a rule of law for ballpark backstops.

4. The dissent argued that such a rule "robs the jury" of the ability to consider important circumstances and locks the law in "a position that is certain to become outdated."

## 3 NEGLIGENCE

### 3.3.3 Negligence Per Se

1. Under negligence per se, **liability exists when the defendant violates a statute**.

2. **Presumption of negligence**: in some states, a jury **must presume** negligence when a statute is breached. The defendant is free to rebut. California follows this rule, with a few exceptions.[24]

3. In other states, juries are free to (but need not) **infer** that breach of statute constitutes negligence—e.g., a car doesn't slow down and hits a pedestrian in a crosswalk.

4. Plaintiff can, and usually will, plead both common law negligence and negligence per se.

5. Compliance with a statute is generally not proof of due care.

6. **Statutory purpose doctrine**: for the statute to be relevant, the harm that occurred must have been the type that the statute was intended to prevent. However, statutory purpose can sometimes be unclear, and it may change through time.

7. Dual purpose doctrine: a statute may have more than one narrow purpose.

8. Generally (including Levy): proof of compliance with a statute is **never** proof of due care. Criminal statutes set a minimum of conduct that could be below what we'd call due care. Some cases take the opposing view.

9. A federal statute may preempt what would otherwise be a state cause of action. Types of preemption: explicit, conflict, and field.

### 3.3.4 Statutory Purpose Doctrine: *Wawanesa Mutual Insurance Co. v. Matlock*

To apply negligence per se, the harm in question must be the type of harm the statute aims to prevent.

1. A minor bought cigarettes for another minor, who later dropped the cigarette and caused a fire that led to significant property damage. The insurer sued the first minor's father.

2. The trial court found for the insurer.

3. The appellate court reversed, holding that that the statute in question (preventing people from purchasing tobacco for minors) was meant to protect against the health hazards of tobacco, not the fire hazard, and therefore cannot be used to establish a standard of conduct in this case.

---
[24] Cal. Evid. C. § 669. See course reader p. 11.

### 3.3.5 Interpreting Legislative Intent: *Stachniewicz v. Mar-Cam Corporation*

Negligence per se applies if the legislature intended to prevent the harm in question.

1. A patron injured in bar brawl sued the bar owner. The plaintiff relied on (1) an Oregon statute which prohibits giving alcohol to an intoxicated person and (2) an Oregon regulation that prevents bar owners from allowing disorderly conduct on their premised.

2. The trial court found for the defendant.

3. The appellate court overturned, reasoning that (1) the statute was inapplicable because the brawler was already drunk when he arrived, so there was no way to tell if another drink caused the brawl, but (2) the regulation was intended specifically to protect customers from injury, and therefore can be an appropriate standard for negligence in this case.

### 3.3.6 Statutory Purpose Doctrine II: *Gorris v. Scott*

See *Wawanesa*, above.

1. Several sheep on a ship were swept overboard. The plaintiff sued the shipowner, arguing that the Contagious Diseases (Animals) Act required the shipowner to enclose the sheep in pens of certain dimensions, which the shipowner failed to do.

2. The court found in favor of the shipowner, reasoning that the Act was intended to prevent the spread of contagious diseases, not to prevent sheep from falling overboard.

## 3.4 Cause in Fact

1. Plaintiff must show that the defendant's negligence was a cause in fact of the harm.

2. Traditionally: plaintiff must prove that the harm would not have occurred **but for** the defendant's actions.

3. If there are multiple causes of harm, each can be but-for causes as long as the harm would not have occurred without it.

4. If there are multiple causes of harm, but none alone is a but-for cause, courts can use the **substantial factor test**. See *Northington* below.

5. The biggest different between but-for test and substantial factor test is that under the substantial factor test, it's much more likely to go to a jury.

# 3 NEGLIGENCE

6. **Proximate cause** removes liability when "the connection between the plaintiff's harm and defendant's liability is unforeseeable or so attenuated that public policy precludes liability."[25]

7. When two people are **"acting in concert"** (i.e., trying to do the same thing), and one is the negligent actor, the court can hold both parties liable.

8. *Summers v. Tice*, below: the California Supreme Court adopted the **alternative liability test**: when one of two negligent defendants probably caused a harm, and it has not been shown that it is more likely than not that either caused it, then **each will be held jointly and severally liable for the full amount of the harm**.

    (a) Restatement Second says the alternative liability test applies when there are "two or more" defendants.

    (b) Also think about the effect of Prop 51 on *Summers v. Tice*: not clear whether it applies to these joint tortfeasor cases or not.

9. *Sindell*, below, established **market share liability**: each defendant shall be held liable for the proportion of the judgment represented by its share of the market unless it can demonstrate that it did not manufacture the product that caused the plaintiffs' injuries. This is the case in California, but not in New York.

10. Toxic torts: what to do when there is no harm, but only enhanced risk? One approach: award damages, but to a lesser amount, based on the percent chance of the harm actually occurring. Seond approach (which is the rule in California): the court will not award general damages, but it will award damages for the costs of relevant medical surveillance.

## 3.4.1 Proving Cause in Fact: *East Texas Theatres, Inc. v. Rutledge*

To establish causation, the cause must have been the cause in fact and it must have been foreseeable.

1. At the defendant's movie theater, somebody threw a bottle from a balcony which struck and injured the plaintiff.

2. The jury found the theater liable because it negligently failed to remove "rowdy persons" from the balcony during the game. The appellate court affirmed.

3. The Texas Supreme Court clarified that proximate cause has two elements: (1) cause in fact and (2) foreseeability. The court held that the prosecution failed to show that the injuries would have occurred but for the removal of the "rowdy persons." Reversed.

---

[25] Casebook p. 206.

## 3 NEGLIGENCE

### 3.4.2 Substantial Factor Test: *Anderson v. Minneapolis, St. P. & S. S. M. Ry. Co.*

The substantial factor test creates liability for a defendant whose actions substantially caused the harm but were not the but-for cause.

1. A spark from a railroad started a fire in a bog on one side of the defendant's property. Another unrelated fire was burning on the other side. The fire from the railroad destroyed the defendant's property, and a few days later it joined with the other fire to make one big fire which destroyed the defendant's home.

2. The railroad argued that it cannot be held liable because the defendant's house would have been destroyed by the other fire anyway.

3. The trial court refused to instruct the jury to follow a rule from an earlier case, *Cook*, which held that there is no liability when two fires jointly destroy property. On this basis, the trial court found for the plaintiff. The railroad requested a motion for judgment notwithstanding the verdict, which was denied.

4. On appeal, the Supreme Court of Minnesota held that the trial court was correct in refusing to apply the *Cook* rule and found for the plaintiffs.

5. **Substantial factor test**: if two independent fires join to cause property damage, there is joint liability, even if neither alone is a but-for cause. Redundant causation is not necessary.

6. Courts are split on whether to use the substantial factor test when only one actor is liable. California courts do use it (and reject the but-for test).

### 3.4.3 Substantial Factor Test II: *Northington v. Marin*

1. The plaintiff, a prison inmate, sued the defendant, a prison guard, for circulating rumors that labeled him a snitch and caused other inmates to assault him. Other guards had spread the same rumors.

2. The trial court found that although the defendant's action was not a but-for cause (since the harm would have occurred without his action), his contribution to the harm was nonetheless a **substantial factor**.

3. The Tenth Circuit affirmed: "Multiple tortfeasors who concurrently cause an indivisible injury are jointly and severally liable; each can be held liable for the entire injury."

### 3.4.4 Proof of Harm: *Herskovitz v. Group Health Cooperative of Puget Sound*

Doctors can be held liable for negligently decreasing a patient's life expectancy even if the patient "probably" would not have lived (i.e., the patient's chance of survival was less than 50%).

*3 NEGLIGENCE* 35

1. The plaintiff brought the action on behalf of her husband, a deceased lung cancer patient, against a doctor that negligently failed to diagnose the patient's lung cancer on his first visit, proximately causing his chance of survival to drop from 39 percent to 25 percent. Neither fact was in dispute.

2. The defendant argued that the plaintiff must prove that the patient "probably" would have lived but for the negligence—that is, without the doctor's negligence, the patient's chance of survival must have been more than 50 percent.

3. The trial court granted summary judgment for the defendant on this argument.

4. The Supreme Court of Washington reversed, arguing that any other decision would mean a "blanket release" for doctors' negligence any time the patient's chance of survival was less than 50 percent. The court reasoned that if a defendant's acts have *increased the risk* of harm to the plaintiff, a jury should decide whether the increased risk actually caused the harm in question.

### 3.4.5 Alternate Liability: *Summers v. Tice*

In cases where there are a small number of defendants, only one of them committed the harm, and we don't know which one, **each defendant is alternately liable for the full harm**. The burden of proof shifts to the defendant.

1. The plaintiff and the two defendants were hunting quail. The two defendants shot at a quail in the direction of the plaintiff. The plaintiff suffered injuries, but it's not clear which defendant's shot was the cause.

2. The court held that the burden of proof shifts to the defendants to determine which one of them caused the injury. If they cannot, "each defendant is liable for the whole damage whether they are deemed to be acting in concert or independently."[26]

### 3.4.6 Market Share Liability: *Sindell v. Abbott Laboratories*

In California, when a product injures a plaintiff but the specific manufacturer that created the harmful product cannot be identified, *all* manufacturers of that product can be held liable according to their share of the market for that product.

1. The plaintiff was harmed by DES, a prenatal drug intended to protect against miscarriages but which turned out to pose significant danger to unborn children. The plaintiff did not know which company manufactured the specific drug her mother took, but since several companies manufactured the drug according to the same formula, she sued them all.

---

[26]Another case with joint tortfeasors: *Drabek v. Sabley* above (kids throwing snowballs at cars)

2. The companies won a dismissal at trial on the grounds that the plaintiff could not identify which company caused the harm.

3. The Supreme Court of California considered four theories of liability:

    (a) The *Summers* test: this failed because there are so many defendants (over 200) that it is highly unlikely that any one of them caused this specific injury.

    (b) The "concert of action" theory: if the defendants had acted in concert to cause the injury, they would be equally liable. In this case, there was not sufficient evidence to show that the defendants had a common plan to cause harm (e.g., by conducting inadequate safety tests or giving insufficient safety warnings).

    (c) "Industry-wide" or "enterprise" liability: if an entire industry cooperates on an element of the harm in question—e.g., by delegating safety testing to a trade association—they can be held jointly liable. Here, the fact that DES manufacturers shared testing and promotion methods did not establish industry-wide liability, because (1) there are so many manufacturers and (2) safety standards are mostly regulated by the FDA.

    (d) **Market share liability**—a variation of the *Summers* test: each manufacturer's liability and share of the damages are proportionate to its market share.

4. Relying on the fourth theory, the court reversed, allowing the plaintiff to proceed with her cause of action.

5. Most states have not adopted market share liability.

6. Defendants are allowed prove definitively that they did not contribute to the harm (e.g., if they can show that they did not produce the drug at the time).

7. Some states require defendants to be joined so that a significant share of the market is represented, and that missing market share proportionally reduces the plaintiff's compensation. Usually (but not always) this must be the nationwide market.[27]

### 3.4.7 Toxic Exposure and Uncertain Harm: *Ayers v. Township of Jackson*

Hypothetical injuries from toxic exposure do not impose liability, but courts can award damages for relevant medical monitoring.

1. A town in New Jersey was found to have caused toxic exposure by its "palpably unreasonable" management of a landfill. The plaintiffs did not

---

[27]Casebook p. 229 n. 2.

## 3 NEGLIGENCE

develop any illnesses, but they sought to recover (1) damages for the enhanced risk of future illness due to exposure and (2) regular medical testing for diseases from exposure.

2. The Supreme Court of New Jersey found that the task of litigating hypothetical injuries would unreasonably strain the tort system (although it suggests that the state legislature could pass a remedy that allowed damages if toxic exposure caused a "statistically significant incidence of disease"). On the second claim, it held for the plaintiffs.

## 3.5 Duty and Proximate Cause

1. Most courts speak about duty and proximate cause as separate elements. However, you could probably build a torts system with just one or the other.

2. *Palsgraf*: four justices deal with it as a duty question, and three in dissent view it as a proximate cause problem.

3. Proximate cause: answers the question of whether there should be liability when the defendant's negligence was a cause in fact of the harm. It is akin to duty, where we ask whether the defendant should be immunized from liability.

4. Two views of proximate cause:

    (a) 1. Rigorous analytical meaning: scope of the risk analysis. There are fact situations where we want to limit liability because the actual harm was not one of the foreseeable harms that made us deem the act to be negligence.

    (b) 2. (Levy's preference.) There are certain fact situations where even though the defendant was negligent, and it caused harm, we choose for policy reasons to have no liability. Courts can conclude that defendant was under no duty; in other cases, courts find that a defendant's conduct was not a proximate cause.

5. Intervening superseding events break the chain of causation. Dependent or naturally occurring events do not.

6. Cardozo: "Danger invites rescue."

### 3.5.1 Common Sense: *Atlantic Coast Line R. Co. v. Daniels*

1. Cause and effect are infinite. An act is the proximate cause if it's close enough. Courts and juries have to rely on reason and common sense to judge whether a cause is proximate.

2. Some sources, like the Restatement on Torts, prefer "legal cause."

3. Proximate cause is a tool for protecting defendants.

### 3.5.2 *Palsgraf v. The Long Island Railroad Company*

Duty and proximate cause are two competing frameworks for examining negligence problems.

1. A railroad employee caused a passenger's package to fall. The package turned out to be full of fireworks. It exploded, causing a scale to break and injure the plaintiff.

2. The trial court found negligence. The Court of Appeals here reversed.

3. Cardozo employs a **duty** framework. Negligence requires the defendant to have a duty to the plaintiff. There must be a point in the chain of causation where an actor is no longer liable—otherwise, anybody who jostles someone in a crowd could be liable. To be negligent, the actor must have breached a reasonable standard of care. In this case, however, the railroad employee could not have known that the package was full of fireworks.

4. Andrews, dissenting, employs a **proximate cause** framework. The actor owes a duty of care to the public at large. Ultimately, proximate cause is about expediency, not logic, and judges must rely on common sense. In this case, the defendant's actions were a but-for cause of the plaintiff's injuries. It's not possible to say that plaintiff's injuries "were not the proximate result of the negligence."

### 3.5.3 Directness vs. Foreseeability: *Overseas Tankship (U.K.) Ltd. v. Morts Dock & Engineering Co. (The Wagon Mound)* Privy Council

Defendants are not liable if the harm was not a **foreseeable consequence** of their negligence.

1. The plaintiffs' ship, the *Corrimel*, was moored for repairs. The appellants' ship, the *Wagon Mound*, was moored nearby. The crew of the *Wagon Mound* accidentally spilled a large amount of oil into the bay. They left soon after without cleaning up the oil.

2. The plaintiff checked with the manager of the wharf where the *Wagon Mound* was moored to see if the oil on the water was flammable. They agreed it was not. Soon after, a small drop of molten metal from the plaintiffs' worked ignited the oil, severely damaging the *Corrimal* and the wharf.

3. *In re Polemis* dealt with another scenario involving fire and negligence. Although the fire was not a foreseeable consequence of the negligence, it was clear that the defendant's action was the direct cause, and the court held for the plaintiffs.

## 3 NEGLIGENCE

4. The court here replaced the direct test from *Polemis* with a foreseeability test.

5. The defendants could not have foreseen a massive fire to be the result of their negligence. Ruling for the defendants.

6. *Kinsman*: foreseeability is a weaker requirement when the consequences are direct and the damage is of the same sort that was risked.[28]

### 3.5.4 Intervening Events: *Thomas v. United States Soccer Fedn.*

Superseding intervening events break the chain of causation.

1. The plaintiff suffered injuries when a soccer game turned violent. He sued the soccer federation for failing to provide a properly trained referee and failing to maintain a safe playing environment. The defendants moved for a summary judgment on the grounds that the alleged negligence was not the proximate cause.

2. The court held that when an intervening act occurs, liability will turn on whether the defendant should have foreseen the act as a consequence of the negligence. It reversed the lower courts and granted the motion for dismissal.

3. "Superseding intervening forces are those new forces which are extraordinarily unexpected."[29]

4. Intervening criminal acts are generally found to be unforeseeable and therefore superseding.

5. "Dependent" intervening forces are results of the defendant's action (e.g., an ambulance driver's collision while rushing to the scene of the defendant's accident). "Independent" intervening forces do not have a causal connection to the defendant (e.g., a lightning bolt).

6. "...ultimately the determinative issue is whether or not the intervening force is extraordinarily unexpected."[30]

### 3.5.5 Uncertainty of Foreseeability *Bigbee v. Pacific Telephone and Telegraph Co.*

Whether a harm is foreseeable is often a jury question.

1. Plaintiff was inside a telephone booth. He saw a car approaching, and he claimed he tried to get out but couldn't. He alleged the telephone booth company was negligent in (1) its manufacture of the booth, which

---
[28] Casebook p. 258.
[29] Casebook p. 261.
[30] Casebook p. 263.

prevented his escape, and (2) its placement in proximity to a busy street, where damage from an oncoming car was foreseeable.

2. The lower courts granted and upheld a motion to dismiss.

3. Here, the Supreme Court of California held that a jury could find that the danger was reasonably foreseeable.

4. Unlikely intervening events are often not found to be superseding events. For instance, if an owner leaves the keys in her car in a high crime area, she may be liable for the harm the car thief causes. (But generally, car owners are not responsible for the actions of car thieves.)

### 3.5.6 The Egg-Shell Plaintiff Rule: *Steinhauser v. Hertz Corporation*

Extra-sensitive plaintiffs can recover full damages.

1. The plaintiff was involved in a car accident. She suffered no injuries, but the accident triggered serious schizophrenia.

2. The court held that as long as there is a causal relationship between the small accident and the catastrophic result, the defendant can be held liable for the "precipitating cause." The probability that the condition would have developed is not a defense, but it can be considered in fixing damages.

3. The large injury from the small cause need not be foreseeable.

## 3.6 Proof of Negligence: Res Ipsa Loquitur

1. **Res ipsa loquitur**: "the thing speaks for itself."

2. It usually has three requirements (with variations among jurisdictions):

    (a) The accident would not have occurred without negligence.

    (b) The negligent act was within the actor's control.

    (c) The plaintiff was not at fault (i.e., no contributory negligence).

3. Res ipsa loquitur is a special kind of circumstantial evidence that allows a jury to find fault without any additional evidence.

4. It's an expansion of the common sense **cookie jar** idea: if a parent returns to see a child next to a broken cookie jar, it's reasonable to infer that the child broke the cookie jar.

5. We can generally assume that a car in motion that hits a pedestrian was negligent—you don't need res ipsa loquitur to show negligence.

## 3  NEGLIGENCE

6. If there is no evidence of res ipsa loquitur, the question is whether the state is a **presumption state or an inference state**. If it's a presumption state, the plaintiff can receive a directed verdict on the presumption of negligence. In an inference state, the jury is free to draw the inference of negligence or not.

7. If the defendant presents evidence of due care, then in all jurisdictions the question would go to a jury.

8. If one of the three conditions is undercut, the jury is given the "conditional res ipsa" instruction: if you find A, B, and C, there is a presumption of negligence.

9. Some courts have relaxed the requirement that the defendant must have had exclusive control of the accident.[31]

10. Some courts follow the *Ybarra* rule (below), which expands the res ipsa loquitur doctrine to medical cases with multiple defendants, where multiple defendants did not have exclusive control of the accident and not all of them were necessarily negligent. It's an extension of the situation where a teacher punishes the entire class for breaking the goldfish bowl.

11. Classic examples where res ipsa loquitur would apply: passenger sitting awake in a train car at the time of a collision; person walking down the street and hit by a falling object.

12. Cal. Evid. Code § 646 establishes a res ipsa loquitur presumption unless the defendant introduces evidence supporting a finding that he was not negligent or that his actions did not proximately cause the harm.

### 3.6.1  Flying Bodies: *Krebs v. Corrigan*

Res ipsa loquitur exists to deal with cases where only the defendant knows the details of the negligent act.

1. The defendant inexplicably flew through the air and landed on the plaintiff's plexiglass sculpture, destroying it.

2. The trial court granted the defendant's motion for a directed verdict.

3. "...human bodies do not generally go crashing into breakable personal property," said the appellate court.

4. Defendant argued (1) that res ipsa loquitur does not apply when the instrumentality is a human body and (2) the doctrine does not apply because there was an eyewitness. The court rejected both of these arguments.

5. The appellate court held that the evidence was sufficient to raise an inference of negligence, so it reversed the directed verdict for the defendants.

---
[31] Casebook p. 275 n. 4.

### 3.6.2 *Ybarra v. Spangard*

Where negligence clearly occurred, but where the responsible defendant is unknown, the plaintiff can rely on res ipsa loquitur.

1. The plaintiff underwent surgery for appendicitis. During the procedure, he suffered a shoulder injury that caused paralysis and muscle atrophy. The plaintiff sued several of the nurses and doctors involved, without knowing who specifically was responsible for the injury.

2. The trial court entered a judgment of nonsuit for all defendants.

3. The plaintiff argued that the doctrine of res ipsa loquitur should apply to the defendants, all of whom were involved at different stages of his medical care.

4. The defendants argued that the plaintiff cannot show that any single defendant caused the injury.

5. As in *Krebs*, the court noted that the purpose of the res ipsa loquitur doctrine is to address cases where the circumstances of the negligence were unknown to the plaintiff (in this case, because he was unconscious).

6. Res ipsa loquitur cases "raise the inference of negligence, and call upon the defendant to explain the unusual result."[32]

7. It could be found in this case that some of the defendants were liable and others are absolved. But that should not preclude the application of res ipsa loquitur. It would not be reasonable to ask the plaintiff to identify which of the individual defendants were responsible for the harm.

8. The defendants' argument would undermine the rights of patients to recover for injuries suffered while unconscious.

9. Judgment of nonsuit was reversed.

## 3.7 Limitations on Duty

1. There is generally no duty to affirmatively act, with a few exceptions:

    (a) One who causes injury may have a duty to rescue.

    (b) The relationship between plaintiff and defendant may create a duty: common carrier, innkeeper, land owners, one who is required or voluntarily takes custody of another to deprive the other of normal opportunities for protection.[33]

    (c) Beginning an undertaking that places the victim in a position that makes them less likely to be rescued can lead to liability.

    (d) Good Samaritan statutes protect from liability.

---

[32] Casebook p. 279.
[33] Casebook pp. 288-89.

## 3 NEGLIGENCE

### 3.7.1 Status and Duty: *L. S. Ayres & Co. v. Hicks*

Legal status can create a duty to act.

1. Hicks, a six-year-old boy, injured his fingers in the escalator at a department store.

2. There is generally no legal duty to act. However, special relationships—master-servant, inviter-invitee, etc.—can give rise to legal duties.

3. The court held that in this case the injury itself was unforeseeable and therefore there is no liability. However, the defendant's status as an inviter established a duty to rescue. The plaintiff was entitled to recover to aggravation of his injuries (but not for the initial injury).

### 3.7.2 Voluntary Interventions: *Miller v. Arnal Corp.*

There is generally no duty to act, but voluntary undertakings can create liability if the person giving aid puts the victim in a worse position.

1. Miller was caught in a snow storm on a mountain. The ski patrol planned to rescue him, but the manager refused to operate the lift because of the danger from the weather. The county sheriff's rescue party reached Miller several hours later after he had suffered severe hypothermia.

2. Miller argued that the attempted rescue put him in a worse position.

3. The court held that Miller did not rely on the ski patrol's planned rescue efforts, nor did the patrol's plan delay the sheriff's rescue.

### 3.7.3 Parental Duty: *Wells v. Hickman*

Parents generally have no duty to control their children unless the parent knows or should know that harm is possible.

1. Hickman's son, D.E., killed Wells' son, L.H. Wells argued that Hickman should be liable for failing to control her son.

2. The court held that "a duty attaches when there has been a failure to control [the child] and the parent knows or should have known that injury to another was reasonably foreseeable."[34]

3. The court held that Hickman did not have a duty to exercise control over L.H. because the harm to D.E. was not foreseeable.

---

[34] Casebook p. 300.

### 3.7.4 Therapists and Potential Victims: *Tarasoff v. The Regents of the University of California*

The relationship between the defendant and a third party can create a duty to a stranger.

1. Moore was a Berkeley psychologist. Poddar, his patient, confided his intention to kill Tarasoff. At Moore's request, the police briefly detained Poddar but released him soon after. Two months later, he did kill Tarasoff.

2. The plaintiffs argued that Tarasoff's death "proximately resulted from defendants' negligent failure to warn Tatiana [Tarasoff] or others likely to appraise her of her danger."[35]

3. The court held that duty (and hence liability) only exists when there is a special relationship between the defendant and the dangerous person or the potential victim. Therapists owe a duty not just to their patients but also to potential victims of their potential actions.

4. "Most therapists are instructed to give so-called '*Tarasoff* warnings' in appropriate cases."

### 3.7.5 Police Duty to the Public: *Davidson v. City of Westminster*

There is no status relationship that creates a duty for police to apprehend a suspected felon or to warn a potential victim. "...police officials generally have no duty to the public."[36]

1. A man had been serially stabbing women in laundromats. One night, Davidson was in a laundromat. Police officers were watching the laundromat when a man they suspected to be the stabber entered. The officers did not intervene and Davidson was stabbed.

2. The court held that the officers did not have a duty to stop the suspected assailant. The police would only have a duty to Davidson if they created her peril, which they did not, so there was no duty to warn her.

## 3.8 Emotional Distress

1. At common law, there was no recovery for emotional distress unless there was physical contact. Bystanders could not recover.

2. Although rejected in California in *Dillon*, the *Amaya* rule allowed those in the "zone of danger" to recover.[37] A slight majority of courts still adhere to the zone of danger rule.

---

[35] Casebook p. 306.
[36] Casebook p. 318 n. 1.
[37] Casebook p. 333 n. 2.

## 3 NEGLIGENCE

3. The *Dillon* factors provided *guidelines* for recovery:

   (a) Was the plaintiff at or near the scene?
   
   (b) Was the distress caused by sensory and contemporaneous observance?
   
   (c) Did the plaintiff have a close relationship with the victim?
   
   (d) (*Dillon* required physical injury or manifestation of emotional distress, but California courts have now eliminated this requirement.)

4. In *La Chusa*, the California Supreme Court turned the *Dillon* guidelines into *requirements* (a "jurisprudence of categories").

5. The *Dillon* approach is becoming a majority view. Some jurisdictions allow non-visual perception of the accident or perception of its aftermath. The "close relationship" requirement generally includes only blood relatives and family members. California recently extended it to include domestic partners. Most *Dillon* jurisdictions require a physical manifestation of the emotional distress, e.g., a heart attack or stomach pains, but not crying or insomnia.[38]

### 3.8.1 Three Factors for NIED Recovery: *Thing v. La Chusa*

The court changed the *Dillon* guidelines into requirements for recovery for negligent infliction of emotional distress.

1. The mother of a child struck by a car sued the driver for negligent infliction of emotional distress (NIED).

2. The trial court granted a summary judgment for the defendant.

3. The appellate court reversed, holding that the mother may recover.

4. The California Supreme Court reversed the appellate court, holding that the trial court was correct in granting summary judgment.

5. In *Amaya v. Home Ice, Fuel, & Supply Co.*, the court held that plaintiffs must have been within the "zone of danger" to recover NIED damages.

6. Five years later, the court overruled *Amaya* in *Dillon v. Legg*. In that case, the mother of the victim may have been endangered by the defendant's conduct, but the sister was not, leading to an incongruous result from the "zone of danger" test. The court held that recovery should be based on the traditional tort principles of foreseeability, proximate cause, and consequential injury. The *Dillon* framework considered three factors:

   (a) Whether the plaintiff was **located near the scene**.
   
   (b) Whether the plaintiff's shock resulted from the emotional impact of **"contemporaneous observance"** of the incident.

---

[38]Casebook pp. 334–336.

## 3 NEGLIGENCE

(c) Whether the plaintiff and victim are **closely related**.

7. Under *Dillon*, the jury will decide on a case-by-case basis "what the ordinary man under such circumstances should reasonably have foreseen."[39]

8. The court here argued that *Dillon* created massive uncertainty. The court replaced *Dillon* with a new rule for finding NIED, which requires three factors:[40]

    (a) Plaintiff must be **closely related** to the victim.
    (b) Plaintiff must be **present at the scene** and aware that an injury has occurred.
    (c) Plaintiff must suffer **emotional distress beyond that which would be anticipated in a disinterested witness**.

9. The court's motivation was to "limit liability and establish meaningful rules for application by litigants and lower courts."[41] Policy reasons included guarding against fraudulent claims and limiting defendants' liability.[42]

10. The dissent argued that *Dillon* was meant to be a flexible test based on the basic principles of torts The court here has replaced it with an arbitrary rule. The "policy reasons" for replacing the foreseeability requirement are not convincing.

11. NIED was originally limited to cases where the plaintiff was physically impacted, i.e., for emotional distress associated with personal injuries. Virtually all courts have abandoned this rule.[43]

### 3.8.2 Fear of Disease from Toxic Exposure: *Potter v. Firestone Tire and Rubber Co.*

NIED recovery for toxic exposure is allowed only if the plaintiff has more than a 50% chance of developing a disease. A 30% chance is not recoverable.

1. Several landowners lived near a landfill, where it was discovered that Firestone had negligently disposed of its toxic waste. The landowners experienced prolonged exposure to carcinogens, and "each faces an enhanced but unquantified risk of developing cancer."[44]

2. The plaintiffs sued for the emotional distress of the fear of developing cancer in the future from exposure to carcinogens.

---

[39]Casebook p. 325.
[40]Casebook p. 323.
[41]Casebook p. 329.
[42]Casebook p. 324.
[43]Casebook p. 333.
[44]Casebook p. 337.

*3 NEGLIGENCE* 47

3. The court held that plaintiffs can recover for negligent infliction of emotional distress from exposure to carcinogens if (1) the defendant's negligence caused the exposure and (2) it is **more likely than not** that the plaintiffs will develop cancer.

## 3.9 Wrongful Death and Survival Actions

1. At common law, there was no recovery for wrongful death or survival actions.

2. Certain named categories of relatives can recover for **wrongful death**. In all but a few jurisdictions, **damages are limited to pecuniary losses, not including pain and suffering**. However, **in California, survivors can collect for monetary value of loss of companionship**—a way of softening the effect of not allowing pain and suffering. A small minority of states also allow recovery for grief.

3. Only certain close relatives can pursue wrongful death actions. See C.C.P. § 377.60 below. Adopted children generally cannot recover for the deaths of biological parents. Courts vary on whether parents can recover for the wrongful death of an unborn child.

4. **Survival actions** are the victim's tort claims that survive the victim. The victim's heirs can pursue those claims in court. Most jurisdictions, including California, **only allow survival of claims for economic losses, not pain and suffering**.

5. Wrongful death

### 3.9.1 C.C.P. § 377: Wrongful Death and Survival Actions in California

1. **Survival Actions** (§ 377.20): (a) A cause of action for or against a person survives that person's death. (b) This section applies even if the loss occurs simultaneously with or after the person's death. (For example, if a driver negligently causes a car accident and dies, the other driver can recover from the negligent driver's estate.)

2. **Damages in Survival Actions** (§ 377.34): recovery is limited to loss incurred before the victim's death.

3. **Wrongful Death** (§ 377.60(a)–(c)): These people can bring wrongful death actions:

   - (a) The decedent's spouse, domestic partner, children, grandchildren, or whoever would be entitled to the decedent's property.
   - (b) Other dependents of the decedent: putative spouse, children of the putative spouse, stepchildren, or parents.

## 3 NEGLIGENCE

- (c) A minor if the minor resided with the decedent for more than 180 days prior to the death and relied on the decedent for half or more of the minor's support.

4. **Wrongful Death Awards** (§ 377.61): Any "damages may be awarded that, under the circumstances of the case, may be just," excluding survival actions.

### 3.9.2 Parental Actions for Wrongful Deaths of Children: *Gary v. Schwartz*

A child's potential contribution to the family weighs heavily in calculating damage awards.

1. The defendant's negligent driving killed the plaintiff's sixteen-year-old son. The jury returned $100,510.40 in damages for the mother.

2. The defendant moved to set aside the verdict as excessive.

3. The court noted that current wrongful death law warranted the application of a formula in calculating damages: "probable wages of the child less cost of upkeep until the infant would have reached 21 years of age."[45] The court noted that this formula would almost always result in a negative figure. The jury instructions prevented awarding damages for emotional factors. However, the court found that the damages were not excessive because the son "in all likelihood...would have faithfully borne the burden of caring for his mother and in aiding his younger brother, if necessary, upon the completion of his education."[46]

### 3.9.3 Less Valuable Children: *Selders v. Armentrout*

There may be little recovery for children to contribute little to the family.

1. The plaintiffs' three children were killed. The jury awarded damages of $1,500 per child, which covered all pecuniary loss.

2. The appellate court found that all the children had left home when they could support themselves and "had made no contribution of earnings other than to their own support."[47] The court held that damages in wrongful death cases cannot be computed by formula but should be left to a jury, and in this case the jury could have reasonably concluded that the loss to the parents ("including the value of society and companionship") was small.

---
[45] Casebook p. 345.
[46] Casebook p. 348.
[47] Casebook p. 349.

### 3.9.4 Extremely Valuable Children: *Compania Dominicana de Aviacion v. Knapp*

Damages can also be high. The jury has broad discretion.

1. The defendants' plane crashed into an auto body shop, killing two of the plaintiffs' three sons. For one of the sons, the jury awarded $1.8 million in damages.

2. The appellate court held that the standard of review does not allow an appellate court to alter a jury verdict simply because it disagrees with it. In this case, the court found that the damages (which included loss of services *and* pain and suffering) was large but appropriate.

## 3.10 Loss of Consortium, Wrongful Birth, Wrongful Life

1. "**Loss of consortium** actions compensate the plaintiff for the loss of society and companionship suffered when another person is injured or the relationship is otherwise tortiously disrupted."[48]

    (a) Generally, only spouses (and in California, domestic partners) can recover.

    (b) Recoverable harms include loss of sexual function, companionship, household services, etc. Courts have upheld recovery for misdiagnosis of syphilis which led a spouse to believe the other was having an affair.[49]

    (c) Some states allow for recovery for loss of consortium after death, not just disability.

2. **Wrongful life** allows a child to recover for having been born under certain conditions (but not for the condition itself). California limits recovery to expenses related to the disability (see *Turpin* below). Most states, however, do not allow wrongful life actions.[50] Courts usually allow recovery for children who were negligently injured while fetuses.

3. **Wrongful conception** allows parents to recover for negligent conception of an unwanted but healthy child. Most jurisdictions allow it.

4. **Wrongful birth** allows parents to recover for negligently causing the birth of a child with a health disability (but not for the disability itself). Many courts allow recovery for the costs of the pregnancy and of raising a disabled child.

---
[48] Casebook p. 364.
[49] Casebook p. 365.
[50] Casebook p. 373–74.

### 3.10.1 Loss of Consortium: *Borer v. American Airlines, Inc.*

Only spouses (and in California, domestic partners) can recover for loss of consortium. Children cannot recover for the loss of consortium of parents.

1. The plaintiffs' mother was disabled when a roof collapsed in an airline terminal.

2. In *Rodriguez*, the California Supreme Court held that loss of consortium covered "loss of love, companionship, society, sexual relationships, and household services" between spouses.[51] The question before the court in this case was whether children can recover for loss of consortium from their parents.

3. The court held that loss of consortium should not extend to the parent-child relationship because (1) monetary compensation is "essentially unrelated" to theloss of "maternal guidance" and (2) loss of parental consortium is "very difficult to measure."[52]

4. In parent-child relationships, loss of consortium is distinct from wrongful death in two ways: (1) without a wrongful death cause of action, it was rational for the defendant to kill the victim rather than inflict injury, and (2) the consequences of a parent's disability can be relieved through the parent's own cause of action.

### 3.10.2 Wrongful Life: *Turpin v. Sortini*

A child born with a hereditary condition resulting from a doctor's negligence cannot recover general damages, but she can recover special damages for expenses relating to her condition.

1. The Turpins brought their first child to have Dr. Sortini examine her for a possible hearing defect. Sortini told them her hearing was within normal limits when, in fact, she was completely deaf. Relying on that diagnosis, the Turpins had another child before learning that their first child was completely deaf and that the deafness was a hereditary condition. Their second child was also born completely deaf.

2. The Turpins sued on behalf of their second daughter to recover (1) general damages for the right to be born without deafness and (2) special damages for medical expenses, teaching, etc.

3. The question before the California Supreme Court was whether a child born with a hereditary condition can recover from a doctor who negligently failed to advise the parents of the possibility of the condition.

---

[51]Casebook p. 360.
[52]Casebook p. 361–62.

## 3 NEGLIGENCE

4. The court held that the daughter could not recover for general damages, but she "may recover special damages for extraordinary expenses necessary to treat the hereditary ailment."[53]

### 3.11 Land Occupiers' Duty

1. Landowners and occupiers (e.g., tenants in possession) traditionally owe no duty of care to visitors to the land.

2. The landowner or occupier's duty depends on the legal status of the visitor. There are three types:[54]

    (a) **Trespassers**: need not have explicit consent. Historically, trespassers have very little protection, except in cases of intentional or willful injury. Some jurisdictions, and the Restatement (Second), impose a reasonable person standard of care on landowners when trespassers or present or should reasonably be anticipated to be present.

    (b) **Invitees**: entering for business purposes or when the land is open to the public. The landowner **must act reasonably to ensure safe conditions for invitees** (although he only needs to act as a reasonable person would—he does not need to eliminate all risks). There is therefore no limit on the landowner's duty to invitees.

    (c) **Licensees**: entering with permission or privilege, e.g., a social guest, or firefighters and police. Licensees traditionally receive very little protection, but today many jurisdictions require the landowner to act reasonably (as with trespassers). Many also require the landowner to warn of concealed conditions posing an unreasonable risk, but not of obvious dangers.

3. Some jurisdictions reject the trespasser's status as the basis of duty, i.e., they treat trespassers, licensees, and landowners alike. Others keep a special category for trespassers.

4. Courts weigh several factors (from *Rowland*, below) in determining when a land occupier has a duty of care:

    (a) Foreseeability of the harm.
    (b) Degree of certainty of the harm.
    (c) Closeness of the connection between the landowner's conduct and the plaintiff's harm.
    (d) Policy of preventing future harms.
    (e) Burden of the duty rule on the defendant.
    (f) Availability of insurance.

5. Child trespassers are often granted special protections.[55]

---

[53] Casebook p. 373.
[54] Casebook pp. 381–82.
[55] Casebook p. 387.

### 3.11.1 Merging Trespassers, Licensees, and Invitees: *Rowland v. Christian*

A landowner's general duty of care to visitors overrides the traditional immunities based on common law classifications (trespasser, licensee, invitee).

1. Nancy Christian had contacted her building manager about a broken bathroom faucet. Rowland was a social guest. She did not warn him about the broken faucet. While using the bathroom, the faucet broke in his hand, causing injuries. He sued for negligence. It was not clear from trial whether the crack in the faucet handle was obvious or concealed.

2. Christian won summary judgment at trial.

3. The California Supreme Court found that a jury could have determined that Christian was aware of the broken faucet, that she should have expected that Rowland would not have discovered the danger, that she did not eliminate the danger or warn him of it, and he did not know or have reason to know of the danger. Summary judgment was therefore inappropriate.

4. Landowners traditionally did not owe a special duty to licensees. However, the traditional classifications of licensee, trespasser, and invitee do not hold up well. Several factors (see above) can alter the traditional rules of duty between the landowner and the visitor.

5. "...everyone is responsible for an injury caused to another by want of his ordinary care or skill in the management of his property." Common law classifications do not warrant "wholesale immunities."[56]

### 3.11.2 Duty and Foreseeability: *Ann M. v. Pacific Plaza Shopping Center*

A landlord's duty depends on the foreseeability of harm. A shopping center's general duty to maintain and control its land in a reasonably safe condition does not require it to provide security guards.

1. Ann M. worked at a photo store in a strip mall. A man entered the store and raped her.

2. Ann M. sued Pacific Plaza for negligently failing to provide adequate security to protect against unreasonable harm.

3. The trial court granted summary judgment on the grounds that Pacific Plaza owed her no duty of care. The appellate court affirmed on the grounds that Pacific Plaza *did* owe a duty, but that no reasonable jury could have concluded that Pacific Plaza acted unreasonably in failing to provide security patrols.

---

[56] Reader p. 20.

# 3 NEGLIGENCE

4. The California Supreme Court held that landlords generally owe a duty to tenants to secure common areas against foreseeable criminal acts of third parties. Here, however, "violent criminal assaults were not sufficiently foreseeable to impose a duty on Pacific Plaza to provide security guards in the common areas."[57] **Courts must balance the foreseeability of the harm against the burden of the duty to be imposed.** The lack of similar prior incidents indicated unforeseeability. Affirmed.

### 3.11.3 Affirming *Ann M.*: *Wiener v. Southeast Childcare Ctrs., Inc.*

Affirming *Ann M.*, criminal acts must be foreseeable to create a duty for a landowner to take additional steps to prevent them.

1. Abrams drove his car through a fence at Southeast Childcare, killing to children. The children's parents sued the childcare center for "provid[ing] inadequate protection [a four-foot-tall chain link fence] against intrusion into the child care center."[58]

2. The trial court granted summary judgment, holding that Abrams's rampage was "wholly unforeseeable." The appellate court reversed on the grounds that an errant motorist careening through the fence was foreseeable.

3. The California Supreme Court held that the "defendants owed no duty to plaintiffs because Abrams's brutal criminal act was unforeseeable."[59] Reversed.

## 3.12 Negligent Misrepresentation and Economic Loss

1. Courts are generally hesitant to award damages for pure economic loss. Damages must usually arise from personal injury or property damage. "In essence, there is no legal duty under negligence to refrain from causing pure economic loss."[60]

2. Under the Restatement (Second) definition, **negligent misrepresentation** occurs when a defendant supplies false information if the plaintiff justifiably relied on it.[61]

3. Most courts require a business relationship between the parties for recovery for negligent misrepresentation.

---
[57] Reader p. 28.
[58] Reader p. 28.
[59] Reader p. 36.
[60] Casebook p. 405.
[61] Casebook p. 406.

## 3 NEGLIGENCE

4. The Second (Restatement) view allows third party recovery if the information provider intended to supply them with the information or knows the recipient intends to use it for a similar transaction.

5. **Most courts do not allow recovery of pure economic loss beyond misrepresentation in business or professional relationships.** *J'Aire*, below, is unusual.

### 3.12.1 Negligent Misrepresentation: *Bily v. Arthur Young & Co.*

Third parties can recover for negligent misrepresentation if they were among the information provider's intended beneficiaries.

1. Plaintiffs invested in the Osborne Computer Company. Osborne hired Arthur Young to handle its accounting. Plaintiffs alleged negligent mispresntation in Arthur Young's audit statement, claiming that the audit stated a slim operating profit when in fact the operating loss was more than $3 million, and that Arthur Young discovered material weaknesses in the company's accounting controls but failed to report them. The plaintiffs won on a general negligence rule.

2. The California Supreme Court here weighed three approaches to negligent misrepresentation:

    (a) **Privity**: Cardozo in *Ultramares* held that auditors are only liable to third parties with a relationship to the auditor "akin to privity."[62]

    (b) **Foreseeability**: Third parties can recover from the auditor if their reliance on the audit was foreseeable.

    (c) **Intended beneficiaries**: The Restatement (Second) holds that third parties can recover from the auditor if they justifiably rely on the audit.

3. The court adopted the intended beneficiaries rule. Reversed.

### 3.12.2 Economic Loss: *J'Aire Corp. v. Gregory*

Contractors are liable to tenants if their work causes foreseeable injury to a tenant's business.

1. J'Aire operated a restaurant at the Sonoma County Airport. Gregory was contracted to do construction work, which it failed to complete in a timely fashion. J'Aire claimed the delays caused it to lose customers. Gregory won a demurrer.

---
[62] Casebook p. 399.

## 3 NEGLIGENCE

2. The California Supreme Court held "that a contractor owes a duty of care to the tenant of a building undergoing construction work to prosecute that work in a manner which does not cause undue injury to the tenant's business, where such injury is reasonably foreseeable."[63] The court strongly emphasized the foreseeability requirement. Reversed.

### 3.13 Comparative Negligence

1. Under **contributory negligence**, a plaintiff who acted at all negligently is barred from recovery.

2. Under **comparative negligence**, the plaintiff's recovery is reduced according to his fault. Under *modified* comparative negligence, the plaintiff cannot recover if she is more than 50% at fault, while *pure* comparative negligence allows a plaintiff who is 99% at fault to recover 1%.

3. Courts must compare the plaintiff's fault to the fault of *all actors*, regardless of whether they are parties to the suit.

4. Exculpatory clauses in contracts require a plaintiff to waive the right to sue for certain injuries. California courts have held that liability for gross negligence is not waivable.

5. **Last clear chance** doctrine: even if the plaintiff was negligent, if the defendant had the last clear chance to avert the harm, the plaintiff could recover.

6. **Assumption of risk** is an implied and knowing waiver of liability for damages the defendant causes. The party assuming the risk must have foreseen it with a high degree of specificity. In *Li*, the California Supreme Court awkwardly tried to distinguish between reasonable and unreasonable risks. Later, in *Knight*, the court revised the assumption of risk rule to distinguish two types:

    (a) **Primary assumption of risk**: the defendant did not breach a duty of care to the plaintiff. The plaintiff is barred from recovery.

    (b) **Secondary assumption of risk**: the defendant *did* breach a duty of care to the plaintiff. The plaintiff's fault is merged into comparative fault.

7. In California, there is no comparative negligence if the defendant's conduct was intentional. Comparative negligence applies if the defendant's conduct was merely willful, wanton, or reckless.

8. Calculating liability under comparative negligence (this approach changes after Proposition 51 (below)): X suffers $100,000 in damages. If X was 40% at fault, the award is reduced by $40,000.

---

[63] Casebook p. 411.

9. **Firefighter's rule**: firefighters and police ordinarily cannot recover for negligence in the course of their jobs because they have assumed the inherent risks in their employment. So, for instance, a firefighter cannot sue a homeowner for negligently setting fire to her home.

### 3.13.1 Pure Comparative Negligence: *Li v. Yellow Cab Co.*

The California Supreme Court replaces contributory negligence with pure comparative negligence.

1. Li made a left turn across traffic, colliding with an oncoming taxi. The trial court found her contributorily negligent and held for the plaintiffs.

2. The California Supreme Court applied the standard of pure comparative negligence, under which Li would be allowed to recover damages minus an amount in proportion to her fault.

3. "In all actions for negligence resulting in injury to person or property, the contributory negligence of the person injured in person or property shall not bar recovery, but the damages awarded shall be diminished in proportion to the amount of negligence attributable to the person recovering."[64]

4. The court reasoned that contributory negligence has a "lottery aspect." "Modified" comparative negligence, which allows plaintiffs to recover if they are less than 50% at fault, only shifts this aspect to a different place.[65] (Most cases use the modified version.[66])

5. The court removed the last clear chance rule, reasoning that it was unnecessary under pure comparative negligence.

6. The court distinguished between "reasonable" and "unreasonable" assumption of risk, holding that unreasonable assumption of risk should be merged into comparative negligence but that reasonable assumption of risk should be retained as a distinct defense. This point proved confusing and the court replaced it in *Knight* with primary and secondary assumption of risk.

7. Previously, the California legislature decided not to adopt a comparative negligence statute. The court believed it had authority on its own to adopt comparative negligence judicially.

### 3.13.2 Assumption of Risk: *Murphy v. Steeplechase Amusement Co.*

You knowingly and voluntarily assume the risk of injury when you get on a ride called The Flopper.

---

[64]Casebook p. 428.
[65]Casebook p. 427
[66]Casebook p. 428.

## 3 NEGLIGENCE

1. Plaintiff fell on "The Flopper" and injured himself. He sued the lift operator for negligence. The trial court found for the plaintiff and the appellate court affirmed.

2. Judge Cardozo: in assumption of risk, the defendant has the burden of proof. To prove the assumption of risk defense, the defendant must prove that the plaintiff took a **knowing and voluntary** risk. The court found that the defendant had proved that the plaintiff assumed the risk knowingly and voluntarily. Reversed.

3. (If the defendant had been contributorily negligent, at the time he would not have been able to recover, because the court had not yet adopted comparative negligence.)

### 3.13.3 Assumption of Risk and Necessity: *Rush v. Commercial Realty Co.*

Necessity negates assumption of risk. Also, check for trap doors in your outhouse. Cf. *Falwell* below.

1. Plaintiff fell through a trap door in an outhouse.

2. The court found that the plaintiff had no choice but to use the outhouse. Therefore, there was no assumption of risk. Affirmed.

3. Cf. *McDermott*.[67] If the plaintiff has no choice in acting, there is no assumption of risk.

### 3.13.4 Thank You Sir, May I Have Another: *Emmette L. Barran, III v. Kappa Alpha Order, Inc.*

Hazing is voluntary.

1. Jones joined a frat. They hazed him. He sued for mental and physical injuries.

2. The court found that Jones knowingly and voluntarily participated, so he assumed the risks of Greek rituals.

### 3.13.5 Assumption of Risk after *Li*: *Knight v. Jewett*

The California Supreme Court clarified assumption of risk under comparative negligence by distinguishing between primary and secondary assumption of risk.

1. Knight and Jewett were at a Super Bowl party. During halftime, they played a game of football with some friends. Knight asked Jewett to stop playing rough. On the next play, he injured her hand and finger. The finger had to be amputated.

---

[67]Casebook p. 437.

## 3 NEGLIGENCE

2. The California Supreme Court replaced the "reasonable" and "unreasonable" assumption of risk distinction from *Li* with primary and secondary assumption of risk:[68]

    (a) **Primary assumption of risk**: the defendant did not breach a duty of care to the plaintiff. The plaintiff is barred from recovery.

    (b) **Secondary assumption of risk**: the defendant *did* breach a duty of care to the plaintiff. The plaintiff's fault is merged into comparative fault.

3. This case therefore turned on whether the defendant breached a duty of care to the plaintiff. The court held that "a participant in an active sport breaches a legal duty of care to other participants—i.e., engages in conduct that properly may subject him or her to financial liability—only if the participant intentionally injures another player or engages in conduct that is so reckless as to be totally outside the range of the ordinary activity involved in the sport."[69]

4. The defendant's conduct did not breach a duty of care to the plaintiff. Therefore, the plaintiff's primary assumption of risk barred recovery.

### 3.13.6 Veterinarian's Rule: *Priebe v. Nelson*

1. Priebe, a kennel worker, sued Nelson when Nelson's dog bit her at the kennel.

2. Priebe claimed she should have won a directed verdict based on strict liability under California's dog bite statute.[70] Nelson argued that the "veterinarian's rule," an application of primary assumption of risk, exempts a dog owner from strict liability to veterinarians.

3. The appellate court found that kennel workers assume the same risk as veterinarians and therefore that recovery should be barred. The California Supreme Court affirmed.

4. However, the strict liability exemption does not apply where the dog owner knew of the dog's violent propensities. If Priebe could show that Nelson had such knowledge, she could prove that he exposed her to an unknown risk, and she would therefore not have assumed the risk.

### 3.13.7 Primary Assumption of Risk in Non-Contact Sports: *Shin v. Ahn*

Primary assumption of risk applies to non-contact sports.

---
[68] Casebook p. 448.
[69] Casebook p. 453.
[70] Cal. Civ. Code § 3342.

## 3 NEGLIGENCE

1. Under the doctrine of primary assumption of risk from *Knight*, sports participants assume the risks inherent in the sport and assume a duty to not increase those risks.

2. Here, an errant golf ball caused serious injury. The court held that the same standard applied to non-contact sports (such as golf). As long as the defendant did not recklessly or intentionally cause the injury, the plaintiff is barred from recovery.

### 3.13.8 Immunity and Government Liability: *Metcalfe v. County of San Joaquin*

Governments are immune by default. Government liability is established by statute.

1. Metcalf was injured in an auto accident. He argued that the city negligently implemented signage in the intersection where the auto accident occurred.

2. The Government Claims Act requires that for a plaintiff to prove that a governmental entity negligently maintained property in a dangerous condition, he must prove that the property was in fact in a dangerous conditions and (1) a government employee created the danger or (2) the government had adequate notice and failed to address the danger.

3. The court held that Metcalf proved neither of the required elements.

4. Governments are immune by default. Governmental liability is based entirely on statute.[71]

5. There are shortened claim statutes and statutes of limitations for suits against the government. For claims against the government, you must submit the claim to a governmental agency within six months. There are then another six months to bring suit. (The general statute of limitations is two years, but not in cases of governmental liability.)

6. Historical immunities from tort liability:

    (a) Charities (until the 50s), because people didn't want donations to be used to pay for suits.

    (b) Intra-family: parents often couldn't sue children and spouses couldn't sue each other.

    (c) Guest statutes: passengers couldn't sue for driver's liability. (Two justifications: (1) not seemly to sue your host and (2) prevents collusion to collect insurance.)

---

[71] The main statute is the CA Government Claims Act.

## 3.14 Joint and Several Liability

1. Defendants who share responsibility for a tort are **jointly and severally liable** for damages, which means each is fully responsible for the entire injury.

    (a) **Joint liability**: multiple parties share liability.

    (b) **Several liability**: liability that is separate and distinct from another's liability.[72]

2. If one person aids or encourages another to cause the injury, the two are **acting in concert**. The assistance must be tortious.

3. If multiple actors committing independent torts cause a single individual injury, all tortfeasors will be held jointly and severally liable.

4. When more than one tortfeasor was available to pay, courts would traditionally divide the payment by the number of defendants (e.g., two defendants would each pay 50%). Courts often now use **comparative indemnification** to allocate damages in proportion to fault.

5. Comparative indemnification is compatible with joint and several liability because if one of the defendants can't pay, the others must fill the gap proportionally.

6. **Contribution** allows a defendant who paid all of the damages to recover from additional defendants who are at fault. By contrast, *indemnification* involves a total shift in liability to a more culpable party.[73]

### 3.14.1 Comparative Indemnity and Cross-Claims: *American Motorcycle Association v. Superior Court*

The California Supreme Court establishes comparative indemnity and the ability for defendants to make cross-claims against any person from whom they seek indemnity.

1. Gregos was injured in a motocross race. He sued the American Motorcycle Association and the Viking Motorcycle Club. AMA cross-claimed against Gregos's parents, alleging the negligently allowed him to participate and seeking indemnification if AMA was found liable.

2. The Supreme Court of California held:

    (a) Comparative negligence does not abolish joint and several liability. "[E]ach tortfeasor whose negligence is a proximate cause of an indivisible injury remains individually liable for all compensable damages attributable to that injury."[74]

---

[72] Black's Law.
[73] Casebook p. 484.
[74] Casebook p. 470.

## 3 NEGLIGENCE

(b) The equitable indemnity doctrine (which divided damages equally among tortfeasors) should give way to partial (or comparative) indemnity, "under which liability among multiple tortfeasors may be apportioned on a comparative negligence basis."[75]

(c) Comparative indemnity is allowed by statute.[76]

(d) Defendants can cross-claim against any person, "whether already a party or not, from whom the named defendant seeks to obtain total or partial indemnity."[77]

3. AMA's cross-complaint was allowed.

### 3.14.2 Proposition 51: Fair Responsibility Act of 1986

1. Prop. 51 **eliminated joint and several liability for non-economic damages**—i.e., defendants are only liable for non-economic damages in proportion to their share of the fault.

2. Defendants are still jointly and severally liable for economic damages.

3. Example: if total non-economic damages are $200,000, and defendant B is 30% liable, the plaintiff can recover $60,000 in non-economic damages from B. If economic damages are $100,000, the plaintiff can still recover the full $100,000 from B.

## 3.15 Insurer's Failure to Settle within Policy Limits

### 3.15.1 *Crisci v. Security Ins. Co.*

Insurers have a duty to protect the interests of their policyholders when considering settlements within the insured's policy limits.

1. Crisci owned an apartment building. One of her tenants slipped through a stairway and sustained severe injuries. Her insurance company litigated the dispute. It rejected settlement offers within the policy limit of $10,000, knowing that if it went to a jury the damages would likely exceed $100,000. The jury did ultimately award damages of $101,000.

2. Crisci brought suit against the insurance company, alleging that it should be liable for an award in excess of its policy limits after failing to accept a settlement offer within its policy limits.

3. The California Supreme Court held that "the test is whether a prudent insurer without policy limits would have accepted the settlement offer."[78] It found that "the evidence is clearly sufficient to support the determination

---

[75] Casebook p. 470.
[76] Casebook p. 471.
[77] Casebook p. 471.
[78] Reader p. 85.

that [the insurance company] breached its duty to consider the interests of Mrs. Crisci in proposed settlements."[79]

4. Barratry

5. Champerty

---

[79]Reader p. 86.

# § 4 Strict Liability

1. **Strict liability**: the plaintiff does not need to prove the defendant's negligence.

2. Applies to abnormally dangerous activities, e.g., transporting gasoline.

3. Abnormally dangerous products (e.g., guns): the fact that a product may be used in an abnormally dangerous way does not hold the manufacturer liable for harms under strict liability. *Kelley*.

4. Strict liability only applies to harms resulting "from that which makes the activity ultrahazardous." *Foster*.

## 4.1 Traditional Strict Liability

1. Strict liability means that the plaintiff's prima facie case does not need to prove that the defendant acted in a blameworthy fashion.

2. Plaintiff has to prove other elements: cause-in-fact, proximate cause.

3. Most important areas: legislative programs (e.g., workers' comp.—not usually referred to as strict liability, but that's how it operates, because fault is generally not an issue), and certain "abnormally dangerous" activities (e.g., keeping wild animals, blasting, use of poisons), strict products liability.

4. An anomaly in the field of torts historically—but liability without fault is present in other areas of the law: contracts (breach of contract generally does not involve fault).

5. Premised on the need for greater loss distribution that what would occur under negligence.

### 4.1.1 Abnormally Dangerous Activities: *Siegler v. Kuhlman*

Strict liability applies to abnormally dangerous activities.

1. Overturned gas trailer caused fire.

2. Transporting gas by truck is abnormally dangerous. It possesses all of the Restatement factors for strict liability.

3. Trial court: defendants overcame charges of negligence.

4. Holding: reversed and remanded for retrial on strict liability.

### 4.1.2 Negligence vs. Strict Liability: *Indiana Harbor Belt Railroad Co. v. American Cyanamid Co.*

1. Cyanamid loaded 20k gallons of acrylonitrile in a leased railroad car.

2. Indiana Harbor Belt asserted (1) negligent maintenance of the train car and (2) strict liability because transport of bulk acrylonitrile through Chicago is abnormally dangerous.

3. Distinction from *Siegler*: defendant there was the transporter; here it is the shipper.

4. Harm here was the result of carelessness, not inherent danger. Negligence would have been an effective deterrent.

5. Reversed and remanded to be tried on negligence.

### 4.1.3 Abnormally Dangerous Products vs. Activities: *Kelley v. R.G. Industries, Inc.*

The fact that a product may be used in an abnormally dangerous way does not hold the manufacturer liable for harms under strict liability.

1. Gunshot victim claimed the manufacturing and marketing of handguns is abnormally dangerous. Court rejected the argument because under SL, the activity must be dangerous in relation to the area where it occurs.

### 4.1.4 Hazard and Causation: *Foster v. Preston Mill Co.*

Strict liability only applies to harms resulting "from that which makes the activity ultrahazardous."

1. Blasting operations caused a mink to kill its kittens. Court rejected the strict liability argument because liability only exists for harms resulting "from that which makes the activity ultrahazardous."

## 4.2 Products Liability

1. A manufacturer (or anyone in the chain of distribution) is strictly liable when an article is placed on the market knowing that it is to be used without further inspection for defects and proves to have a defect that causes injury.

2. Strict liability is not based on fault. The rationale is loss distribution.

3. In addition to strict liability, manufacturers can also be held liable for negligence, express/implied warranty, and representation.

4. Defect is defined as an imperfection that impairs the operation or safety of a product.

5. Issues in defining defect have split jurisdictions:

    (a) Must the product be "unreasonably dangerous"? The majority of states require it, but CA says no, because it introduces a negligence standard. Can there be liability for an open an obvious defect? CA no, others yes.

    (b) Must the product be in a condition not anticipated by the buyer, i.e., beyond the consumer's expectation? Some jurisdictions make this a requirement. In CA, that's one method of getting to strict liability (*Barker*—see the next bullet), but it's not necessary. Some say this introduced negligence, but (1) it's in hindsight, not foresight and (2) the burden of proof is on the defendant, not the plaintiff. But see *Sewell*: if the product is too complex, the consumer expectations test does not apply.

    (c) The *Barker* test: a product is defective if (1) it failed to perform as safely as an ordinary consumer would expect whe used in an intended or reasonably foreseeable manner, or (2) if the benefits don't outweigh the risk of danger inherent in the design.

6. No strict liability for prescription pharmaceuticals.

7. **State-of-the-art defense**: is the defendant relieved of liability if at the time of the manufacture, nobody could have made it more safe. Some states have adopted this rule; in CA it's only adopted in a few areas—pharmaceuticals, warning defects (*Anderson*).

8. Manufacturing defect: the product is different than all the others produced.

9. Warning defect: inadequate labels or instructions. Purposes: inform the consumer of dangers to let her avoid buying it or to use it more safely.

10. Restatement (Third) of torts would radically shift products liability in favor of manufacturers. Plaintiff would have to prove the existence of a reasonable alternative design. The *Potter* court rejected the rule as unduly requiring plaintiffs to retain expert witnesses. No chance that this rule will be adopted in CA in the foreseeable future.

11. Restatement (Third) also tries to combine products liability into a single principle (§ 550.1). Levy fears this would wipe away much of existing products liability law.

12. Strict liability does not allow recovery for economic damages.

13. If plaintiff is negligent, we will apply comparative negligence, even in strict products liability cases. There's dispute about whether fault can logically apply in strict liability contexts.

# 4 STRICT LIABILITY

14. Preemption: when do federal rules preempt state law? There are three types of preemption under the Supremacy Clause: express, conflict, field.

15. Can there be liability for component parts of a product? Cases are not all in agreement. Best rule: (1) if the component part is defective, there can be liability. (2) If the component parts manufacturer was intimately involved in the design of the whole product, it can be held liable for the whole product.

16. The "sophisticated/professional user" defense: a manufacturer generally owes no duty to warn professionals against the danger if the danger is generally known to the profession.

17. *Daly*, comparative negligence: can you apply assumption of risk to a strict products liability case? The answer will likely be yes, though there is no California Supreme Court case that directly addresses it.

18. Focuses on the product itself, not the manufacturer's conduct.

## 4.2.1 Strict Liability for Food and Drugs: *Pillars v. R. J. Reynolds Tobacco Co.*

1. Human toe in chewing tobacco triggered strict liability.

## 4.2.2 Origins of Strict Products Liability: *Greenman v. Yuba Power Products, Inc.*

1. This is the first case to find strict products liability for defective products.

2. A piece of wood flew out of a woodworking tool, the Shopsmith, injuring the plaintiff, Greenman.

3. 10.5 months later, he sued the manufacturer, Yuba, and the retailer for breach of warranty and negligence.

4. The court found that (1) the retailer was not negligent and did not breach an express warranty, and (2) the manufacturer did not breach an implied warranty. Thus, the only valid causes of action were (1) a breach of implied warranty against the retailed and (2) negligence and a breach of express warranty against the manufacturer. The jury found for the retailer and found $65,000 against Yuba.

5. Yuba appealed; Greenman sought appeal against the retailer only if the judgment against Yuba was reversed.

6. The jury could have reasonably found that Yuba negligently manufactured the Shopsmith.[80]

---
[80] Casebook p. 520.

## 4 STRICT LIABILITY

7. The requirement that consumers need not give notice of injury to manufacturers with whom they have not directly dealt. Thus, the plaintiff's cause of action was not barred.

8. The manufacturer can be held strictly liable for a defective product even in the absence of an express warranty: **"A manufacturer is strictly liable in tort when an article he places on the market, knowing that it is to be used without inspection for defects, proves to have a defect that causes injury to a human being."**[81]

9. Liability for defective products is governed by strict liability, not contract warranties.

10. The purpose of strict liability for defective products is to ensure that manufacturers bear the costs of injuries to consumers.

11. **Warranties**:

    (a) *Express warranties*: created when the seller makes factual assertions about a product.

    (b) *Implied warranties*: (1) "implied warranty of merchantability" is a guarantee that products conform to their description and are safe for their intended use; (2) "implied warranty of fitness for a particular purpose" is created when the seller has reason to know that the buyer buys the goods for a particular purpose. [82]

    (c) The advantage of basing a products liability case on a warranty theory is that liability is strict and there can be compensate for pure economic loss. The disadvantage is that sellers can limit remedies or disclaim warranties altogether. Warranties also historically require prompt notice of dissatisfaction to the defendant.[83]

12. **Misrepresentation**: another theory for product liability (in addition to negligence and warranty theory). It holds manufacturers liable for harm caused by justified reliance on the misrepresentation.

13. **Strict product liability**: a fourth theory. It imposes liability on manufacturers for defective products that proximately cause personal and property injuries. [What about economic injuries?] This is the theory in *Greenman*.

### 4.2.3 No Privity Required: *Lee v. Crookston Coca-Cola Bottling Co.*

Consumers can sue manufacturers directly without involving others in the distribution chain.

---

[81] Casebook p. 521.
[82] Casebook p. 523.
[83] Casebook p. 524.

## 4 STRICT LIABILITY

1. Coke bottle exploded in waitress's hands.

2. Four policy justifications for strict products liability:

    (a) Discourage marketing of defective products.

    (b) Put burden of loss on manufacturer.

    (c) Maximize legal protections for consumers.

    (d) Allow injured parties to bring actions directly against those who caused the injuries without involving others in the distribution chain.

### 4.2.4 Foreseeable Dangers: *Gray v. Manitowoc Company*

Strict liability only applies of the dangers were beyond what an "ordinary consumer" would anticipate.

1. Crane hit construction worker, who argued that mirrors should have been provided. Court found that the safety hazards of this type of crane were well known in the industry and thus was not "dangerous to a degree not anticipated by the ordinary consumer of this product."[84]

### 4.2.5 Tobacco-Related Health Problems: *Roysdon v. R.J. Reynolds Tobacco Co.*

Cigarettes' health risks do not make them defective.

1. Roysdon suffered from tobacco-related health problems. The Sixth Court held that a product that is generally harmful to health is not the same as a product that is defectively manufactured.

2. "...we think that a reasonable jury could not find that that the cigarettes are defective."[85]

3. If the dangers of smoking are *not* **common knowledge**, then a jury *may* be able to find that cigarettes are unreasonably dangerous.

### 4.2.6 Replacing the Consumer Expectations Test: *Barker v. Lull Engineering Co., Inc.*

Products liability does not depend on a consumer's expectation of safety—i.e., it should not be limited to the "unreasonably dangerous" standard where liability would only apply if was less safe than the consumer expected.

1. The plaintiff was injured while operating a high-lift loader. He alleged defective design as the proximate cause.

---

[84]Casebook p. 531.
[85]Casebook p. 534.

## 4  STRICT LIABILITY

2. The court developed a two-prong test for determining whether a productive is defective in design:

   (a) If it fails to perform as safely as an ordinary consumer would expect when used in an intended or reasonably foreseeable manner;, or

   (b) When the benefits of the design do not outweigh the inherent dangers, i.e., if the design embodies "excessive preventable danger."[86]

3. The court rejected the idea that a manufacturer can be held strictly liable only if a product is "unreasonably dangerous," i.e., if it is "more dangerous than contemplated by the average consumer."

### 4.2.7  State-of-the-Art Defense: *Beshasda v. Johns-Manville Products Corp.*

The state-of-the-art defense shields manufacturers from liability if they could not have known of the dangers their product posed at the time of manufacturing. Asbestos is a paradigmatic case. Although New Jersey here rejected the defense, most jurisdictions (including California) allow it.

1. This was a consolidated case against six asbestos manufacturers. The defendants' "state-of-the-art" defense argued that the dangers of asbestos were unknowable at the time the injuries in question occurred.

2. The trial court denied the plaintiffs' motion to strike the state-of-the-art defense.

3. The plaintiffs claimed strict liability for failure to warn. "The issue is whether the medical community's presumed unawareness of the dangers of asbestos is a defense to plaintiffs' claims."[87]

4. The court distinguished negligence, which is conduct oriented, from strict liability, which is product oriented.

5. There is a two-part **risk equity** test to determine whether a product is safe:]

   (a) Does its utility outweigh its risk?

   (b) Has that risk been reduced to the greatest extent possible consistent with the product's utility?[88]

6. In strict liability cases, there is no need to prove that the manufacturer knew or should have known of the product's danger. Knowledge is imputed to the manufacturer. "...in strict liability cases, culpability is irrelevant."[89] The state-of-the-art defense is a negligence defense because it rests on the defendant's conduct.

---

[86]Casebook p. 542.
[87]Casebook p. 549.
[88]Casebook p. 551.
[89]Casebook p. 552.

7. There are three reasons for imposing strict liability for failure to warn:
   (a) *Risk spreading*: spreading costs of harm to manufacturers and purchasers is preferable to imposing it on innocent consumers.
   (b) *Accident avoidance*: industries play an important role in safety research, and we want them to maximize it.
   (c) *Fact finding*: the dangers of asbestos *could have been known*, but weren't. Regardless, it's better to leave out the negligence concept of knowability, because the framework here is strict liability, not negligence.

8. The court granted the plaintiffs' motion to strike the state-of-the-art defense.

9. (In contrast to New Jersey, the majority trend is to allow the state-of-the-art defense, including in California.[90])

## 4.2.8 Federal Preemption: *Riegel v. Medtronic, Inc.*

Medical device regulations preempt state tort law actions. The rationale is that states and individual juries should not be able to undermine the FDA's regulatory authority.

1. The Medical Device Amendments (MDA) to the FDCA established various levels of federal oversight for medical devices depending on their risks. Devices that were already on the market were grandfathered, and new devices that were "substantially similar" to the existing devices could also sidestep premarket approval.

2. Here, the doctor inflated a balloon catheter beyond the pressure limit indicated on its label, causing injury to the plaintiff.

3. The district court held (1) that the MDA preempted the plaintiff's common law tort claims and (2) that the MDA preempted the plaintiff's negligent manufacturing claim because it did not claim that the manufacturer violated federal law.[91]

4. Justice Scalia:
   (a) The MDA only preempts state requirements that are different or in addition to the applicable federal requirements. The court here, relying on *Lohr*, found that state law negligence and strict liability claims are different and therefore the MDA preempts them.
   (b) If federal regulations did not preempt state common law, then states and individual juries would be able to undermine the FDA's expert evaluations and policies.

---

[90]Casebook p. 557.
[91]Casebook p. 562.

## 4 STRICT LIABILITY

(c) The consequence is that the FDA's approval of the device preempts state tort law actions based on negligence and strict liability.[92]

### 4.2.9 More Federal Preemption: *McKenney v. PurePac Pharmaceutical*

If the state law cause of action is in *parallel* to the federal cause of action, there is no preemption.

1. PurePac manufactured the generic drug metoclopramide. McKenney claimed she was injured because of "false or misleading statements" in the drug's labeling.[93]

2. The CA Superior Court sustained PurePac's demurrer and entered summary judgment in its favor.

3. In its demurrer, PurePac contended that McKenney's claim was barred by the defense of federal preemption. Because it submitted its labeling to the FDA and won approval, PurePac argued it could not be held liable for state tort law claims regarding any deficiencies in the labeling.

4. *Brown* and *Carlin* affirmed strict tort liability for pharmaceutical manufacturers in California.

5. The court found that FDA approval of labeling does not preempt state tort claims against manufacturers.

6. Reversed (demurrer rejected).

7. Reconciling *Riegel* and *McKenney*: courts will likely allow state causes of action that are parallel to the federal rules.

### 4.2.10 Restatement (Third) Approach: *Potter v. Chicago Pneumatic Tool Co.*

The Restatement (Third) requires plaintiffs claiming design defects to propose a "reasonable alternative design" and holds that a product is defective only if there are foreseeable risks that a reasonable alternative design would have avoided. The court rejected this standard as too onerous for plaintiffs.

1. Plaintiffs claim they were injured from excessive vibrations as a result of defective warnings on the defendant's product.

2. Courts are divided on the definition of design defects.

3. The Restatement (Third) requires plaintiff to prove the existence of a "reasonable alternative design."[94] The defendants argue that the court should adopt this standard.

---

[92] Casebook p. 565.
[93] Casebook p. 89.
[94] Casebook p. 566.

## 4 STRICT LIABILITY

4. The court here reasoned that the Restatement (Third) approach puts an undue burden on plaintiffs by requiring expert witnesses even in cases where a lay jury could infer a design defect. Moreover, cases exist where a product is defective even though no alternative design exists.

5. The Restatement (Third) holds that a product is defective only if there are foreseeable risks that a reasonable alternative design would have avoided. Thus, it allows the state-of-the-art defense and imposes a burden on plaintiffs more onerous than ordinary negligence (because under ordinary negligence, the plaintiff only needs to prove a foreseeable risk, but not the existence of an alternative design).

### 4.2.11 Economic Damages: *Two Rivers Company v. Curtiss Breeding Service*

The court held that plaintiffs cannot recover for economic loss alone under strict liability. However, if there is *also* personal or property injury, there can be recovery for pure economic loss.

1. Plaintiff sued defendant for economic damages from allegedly defective cattle semen.

2. The court distinguished four types of property loss:

    (a) Personal injury to the user or the user's property.

    (b) Pure economic loss. Earlier courts held that **strict liability does not apply to pure economic loss**. Instead, individuals claiming economic loss must claim under UCC breach of implied warranty or common law negligence.

    (c) Economic loss to the purchased product itself.

    (d) Hybrid: harm to the plaintiff's other property as well as to the product itself.

3. The court held that plaintiffs cannot recover for economic loss alone under strict liability. However, if there is *also* personal or property injury, there can be recovery for pure economic loss.

### 4.2.12 Comparative Negligence in Strict Products Liability: *Daly v. General Motors Corp.*

In California, courts can take into account the plaintiff's comparative negligence (*Li*) *does* in actions based on strict products liability.

1. Decedent crashed into a fence along the highway. The door of his Opel was thrown open, causing him to be forcibly ejected from the car. He sustained fatal head injuries. It was undisputed that his injuries would have been relatively minor if he had remained inside the car.

## 4 STRICT LIABILITY

2. Daly was comparatively negligent because he did not use his seat belt or the door lock.

3. Strict products liability in California is based on the "problems of proof" in proving negligence or breach of warranty. Since injured consumers are powerless to protect themselves, it is fair to place the burden of loss on manufacturers.[95]

4. Held: courts can consider a plaintiff's comparative negligence in adjudicating strict liability claims.

### 4.2.13 Applying the *Barker* Test to Component Parts: *Gonzales v. Autoliv*

Component parts manufacturers can be strictly liable for design defects if the benefits of the design do not outweigh the inherent dangers.

1. Gonzalez suffered an eye injury when an airbag manufactured by Autoliv deployed in a minor collision.

2. The court applied the *Barker* test, asking whether the benefits of the product's design outweighed the inherent risks. Autoliv offered no evidence that the benefits outweighed the dangers. Summary judgment for Autoliv was therefore inappropriate.

---

[95]Casebook p. 577.

# § 5 Damages

## 5.1 Compensatory Damages

### 5.1.1 Loss of Enjoyment and Pain and Suffering: *McDougald v. Garber*

1. Nonpecuniary damages compensate a victim for physical and emotional consequences, such as pain and suffering or loss of ability. Pecuniary damages compensate for economic loss.

2. The victim here suffered permanent brain damage and entered a coma after a C-section.

3. After a remittitur, the plaintiff won $2,000,000 for conscious pain and suffering and loss of the pleasures and pursuits of life. Her husband won $1,500,000 for loss of services.

4. The trial court accepted the plaintiffs' argument that damages for loss of enjoyment of life could be awarded even though the plaintiff was not aware of the loss. The appellate court held (1) that awareness is required to recover for loss of enjoyment of life and (2) separating damages for pain and suffering from damages for loss of enjoyment is not possible because suffering and enjoyment cannot be directly converted into monetary values.

5. The purpose of tort damages is to compensate the victim. They should not be punitive unless the defendant acted with malice.[96]

6. Pain and suffering generally encompass loss of enjoyment.[97]

7. Judge Titone, dissenting: Pain and suffering are logically distinct from loss of enjoyment. Damages for each should be kept separate.

### 5.1.2 Collateral Source Rule: *Helfend v. Southern California Rapid Transit District*

1. A bus crushed the plaintiff's arm.

2. At trial, the defendant sought to introduce evidence showing that insurance had paid 80%, possibly more, of the plaintiff's medical bills. The court ruled that the defendants could not show that the plaintiff had received medical coverage from any **collateral source**.

3. On appeal, the defendant argued that the trial court erred in preventing evidence that a collateral source had paid the plaintiff's medical bills and denying the defendant the opportunity to discover whether the defendant had recovered costs from more than one collateral source.

---

[96]Casebook p. 607.
[97]Casebook p. 610.

## 5 DAMAGES

4. The collateral source rule exists to create an incentive for people to buy health insurance. Moreover, attorneys generally draw compensation from damages at trial, which would be put in peril if juries knew the plaintiff had already recovered from an insurance company.

5. Changes to the collateral source rule "would be more effectively accomplished through legislative reform."[98]

6. Subrogation clauses in insurance policies entitle the insurer to tort damages up to the amount the insurer paid.

## 5.2 Punitive Damages

### 5.2.1 *State Farm Mutual Automobile Ins. Co. v. Campbell*

1. The plaintiff, Campbell, tried to pass six cars on the highway. To avoid colliding with the plaintiff, Ospital swerved, killing himself and permanently disabling Slusher.

2. Campbell initially insisted he was not at fault, but a consensus emerged that his attempted pass caused the accident. But State Farm contested liability and declined settlement offers from Slusher and Ospital's estate. State Farm assured the Campbells that their assets were safe, they had no liability, and they did not need to seek outside counsel. When the jury determined that Campbell was at fault and awarded $185,849 in damages, State Farm told the Campbells "to put for sale signs on your property to get things moving."[99]

3. While the appeal was pending, the Campbells struck a deal with Ospital and Slusher to pursue a bad faith action State Farm. Slusher and Ospitals attorneys would represent the three of them, with Slusher and Ospital entitled to 90% of any verdict against State Farm.

4. The jury awarded $145 million in punitive damages and $1 million in compensatory damages against State Farm.

5. The Supreme Court here considered whether the punitive damages were excessive. It noted that compensatory damages redress concrete losses while **punitive damages aim for deterrence and retribution**. Supreme Court here considered whether the punitive damages were excessive and in violation of due process.

6. In *BMW v. Gore*, the Supreme Court established three criteria for reviewing punitive damages:[100]

---

[98] Casebook p. 614. The California legislature did in fact remove the collateral source rule—see *Fein*, p. 629.
[99] Casebook p. 615.
[100] Casebook p. 616.

(a) The reprehensibility of the defendant's conduct.
   (b) The disparity between actual/potential harm and the punitive damages.
   (c) The difference between damages awarded and damages in similar civil cases.

7. Applying the *Gore* criteria, the court found that "this case is neither close nor difficult. It was error to reinstate the jury's $145 million punitive damages award."[101]

8. Four states have abolished punitive damages (Levy).

9. Punitive damages resemble criminal punishment in some respects (e.g., retribution). The burden of proof is lower (preponderance of the evidence vs. beyond a reasonable doubt), but the punishments are purely economic.

### 5.2.2 Cal. Civ. Code § 3294

1. California allows recovery of punitive damages for oppression, fraud, malice, and homicide resulting from a felony.

2. Burden of proof for punitive damages is "clear and convincing evidence."[102]

---

[101] Casebook p. 617.
[102] Reader p. 102.

## § 6 Vicarious Liability

1. Vicarious liability is the doctrine that holds one party liable because of that party's relationship to a tortfeasor.

2. The most common form of vicarious liability is respondeat superior, which hold an employer liable for its employees' torts.

3. You cannot insure for punitive damages.

### 6.1 Respondeat Superior: *Rodgers v. Kemper Construction Co.*

1. Respondeat superior: an employer is liable for an employee's torts committed within the scope of employment.

2. Kemper employees frequently drank after their shifts. Herd and O'Brien finished their shifts, drank a few beers, walked across the job site, and asked Rodgers for a ride on the bulldozer. They beat him up when he refused. Rodgers later asked Kelley to help find out his assailants' identities. As Rodgers wrote down O'Brien's license plate number, Herd, O'Brien, and a third, Dieffenbauch, attacked Rodgers and Kelley, causing serious injury to both.

3. The trial court found Kemper liable for the injuries under respondeat superior.

4. On appeal, Kemper argued that it could not be held liable under respondeat superior because (1) the assault occurred after O'Brien and Herd had finished their shift and (2) the assault was based on personal malice.

5. The appellate court rejected both of Kemper's arguments on the grounds that the injuries resulted from "a dispute arising out of the employment."[103]

### 6.2 Going-and-Coming Rule: *Caldwell v. A.R.B., Inc.*

1. Generally, there is no employer liability for an employee's actions while commuting.

2. A.R.B. workers at a Shell Oil plant were sent home because of bad weather. Brandon offered to give Richardson a ride home. On the way, Brandon collided with Caldwell. Caldwell sued Brandon and A.R.B., alleging that Brandon was acting within the scope of employment. A.R.B. filed a motion for summary judgment on the grounds that Brandon was outside of the scope of employment, which the trial court granted.

---

[103] Casebook p. 636.

3. Although A.R.B. compensated its employees for travel expenses, the appellate court held that Brandon was outside the scope of employment.

## 6.3 Independent Contractors: *Mavrikidis v. Petullo*

1. Gerald Petullo was driving a dump truck full of hot asphalt when he collided with Mavrikidis. Petullo and his father had been working on renovations of the Clar Pine service station, which Karl Pascarello owned,

2. Malvrikidis argued that Petullo was an employee of Pascarello, but the court held that he was an independent contractor. Restatement (Second) of Agency lists several factors for determining whether an actor is an employee.[104] Applying these factors, the court found that Petullo was not an employee.

3. The court listed three exceptions to independent contractor non-liability: (1) when the principal retains control of the work, (2) when the principal hires an incompetent contractor, and (3) when the work is inherently dangerous. None of these exceptions applied to Petullo.

4. Pascarello was not liable.

## 6.4 Vicarious Liability for Children: *Wells v. Hickman*

1. L.H. (15) beat D.E. (12) to death. D.E.'s mother (Wells) filed a wrongful death action against L.H.'s mother (Hickman) and grandparents.

2. An Indiana statute held parents strictly liable for their children's knowing, intentional, or reckless torts for damages up to $3,000. The trial court granted summary judgment for Hickman.

3. The appellate court here reasoned that there are four common law exceptions to the rule that a parent is not liable for a child's torts: (1) when the parent entrusts the child with an instrumentality that may pose danger to others, (2) where the child acts as the parents' agent, (3) where the parent consents, and (4) where the parent fails to exercise control when the parent knows or should know that injury is possible.

4. Wells argued that the Hickman's actions fell under the fourth exception and that the statute did not limit recovery. The appellate court agreed.

---

[104]Casebook p. 647.

## § 7 Tort Reform

### 7.1 *Fein v. Permanente Medical Group*

1. Lawrence Fein felt chest pain and went to his doctor's office, where a nurse practitioner told him that his pain was due to a muscle spasm and sent him home with Valium. The chest pains returned that night. He went to the emergency room, where the doctor also diagnosed the problem as muscle spasms, giving him a Demerol injection and a codeine prescription. The next day, he went back to the emergency room, where an EKG showed he was suffering from a heart attack.

2. Fein sued Kaiser for malpractice, arguing at trial that the failure to initially diagnose his heart attack caused much of his heart muscle to die, reducing his life expectancy by at least 16 years. The trial court awarded $1 million in economic damages.

3. On appeal, Fein argued that the trial court erred in applying two provisions of the Medical Injury Compensation Reform Act (MICRA), (1) limiting non-economic malpractice damages to $250,000 (Cal. Civ. Code § 3333.2) and (2) modifying the collateral source rule in malpractice cases (Cal. Civ. Code § 3333.1.

4. Fein contended that § 3333.2 ($250,000 limit on non-economic damages) denied due process. The court held that the legislature pursued a legitimate statute interest in enacting the statutory limits on recovery. Fein also argued that the limit denied equal protection by discriminating against malpractice victims and against malpractice plaintiffs with non-economic damages above $250,000. The court rejected both arguments.[105]

5. Fein also raised a constitutional challenge to § 3333.1 (allowing collateral source evidence and preventing the collateral source from obtaining subrogation). The court held that although the provision affected a plaintiff's recovery, it was constitutional because it promoted the legitimate state interest of containing health care costs.

6. Affirmed.

### 7.2 Eisenberg and Sieger, "The Doctor Won't See You Now"

Rising insurance costs prompt malpractice recovery reforms.

---
[105] Casebook p. 627.

## 7.3 Treaster and Brinkley, "Behind those Medical Malpractice Rates"

Increases in insurance premiums do not closely correlate with increases in the number of malpractice claims or the size of damage awards. Rather, the increases may be due to unsuccessful insurance company investments.

## 7.4 Colliver, "We Spend Far More, but Our Healthcare is Falling Behind"

U.S. healthcare costs skyrocket while relative quality drops.

## 7.5 Sack, "Doctors Say 'I'm Sorry' before 'See You in Court'"

Disclosing mistakes to patients dramatically reduces malpractice litigation which, in turn, reduces health care costs.

## 7.6 Patient Protection and Affordable Care Act § 6801

The Senate supports exploring alternatives to civil litigation of malpractice disputes.

## § 8 Workers' Compensation

1. Workers' compensation allows employees to recover damages for injuries without needing to prove negligence. The full economic loss is generally not recovered, and compensatory damages for intangibles (e.g., pain and suffering) and punitive damages are generally excluded.[106]

2. The injury must have occured within the scope of employment.

3. *Fellow servant rule*: under common law, contributory negligence of a co-employee is attributed to the injured employee, making it more difficult for the injured employee to sue his employer under negligence.[107]

### 8.1 Immobility Requirement: *Bletter v. Harcourt, Brace & World, Inc.*

You're allowed to dance on the job.

1. A high school textbooks editor was feeling good. He "attempted to do a dance step but fell and fractured his thigh."[108]

2. The workers' compensation board "finds that claimant's casual indulgence in a little dance step on the employer's premises and while in a swiftly moving elevator, was not an unreasonable activity in view of his feeling of well-being created by his liking for both the job and his co-workers, so as to be deemed a deviation from the employment."

3. The court agreed with the board that employees are "not required to remain immobile."

4. Many jurisdictions have an exception for intentional torts. Courts are divided on whether the threshold is desire or substantial certainty.[109]

### 8.2 Off Duty Employees: *Ralphs Grocery v. Workers' Comp. Appeals Bd.*

Employees are not within the scope of employment when they are off duty.

1. Moeller was on disability leave for a finger injury. He also had congenital heart disease. His employer, Ralphs Grocery, laid him off while he was on disability leave, but he was scheduled to return several months later. The night before he wsa scheduled to return, Ralphs called to tell him that his position had been reduced to part time without benefits. Moeller immediately suffered a fatal heart attack.

---

[106] Casebook p. 661–62.
[107] Casebook p. 661.
[108] Casebook p. 657.
[109] Casebook pp. 674–75.

2. The Workers' Compensation Judge found that the call caused Moeller's death and that the call arose in the course of employment, awarding damages to Moeller's widow.

3. The appellate court held that employer-employee relationship is severed while the employee is off duty. Moeller was off duty when he received the call from Ralphs, and therefore he was outside the scope of employment. Reversed.

## 8.3 Special Risk Exception: *Johnson v. Stratlaw, Inc.*

A plaintiff cannot bring a negligence cause of action if the employee was within the scope of employment when the harm occurred. The special risk exception to the going and coming rule puts an employee within the scope of employment.

1. Daryl worked at Stratlw's Straw Hat Pizza Parlor. One evening, Straw Hat required Daryl to work from 5 p.m. to 2 a.m. Daryl died of a car accident while driving home.

2. Daryl's family sued for wrongful death and negligent infliction of emotional distress. Stratlaw demurred that workers' compensation barred negligence actions and that the NIED claim was invalid because the plaintiffs had not witnessed the accident.

3. The trial court sustained the NIED demurrer but overruled on all other grounds. The trial later granted summary judgment on all counts for the defendants.

4. On appeal, plaintiffs argued that Daryl was not within the scope of employment when the accident occurred.

5. The appellate court held that the going and coming rule generally puts the employee outside the scope of employment while commuting. However, the **special risk exception** applies "if (1) 'but for' the employment the employee would not have been at the location where the injury occurred and (2) if 'the risk is distinctive in nature and qualitatively greater than risks common to the public.'"[110]

6. The court held that the special risk exception applied here. Affirmed.

## 8.4 Intentional Torts: *Fermino v. Fedco, Inc.*

In California, workers' compensation does not bar employees' claims against employers for intentional torts.

---

[110]Casebook p. 666.

## 8  WORKERS' COMPENSATION

1. Fermino worked at Fedco's department store. Fedco accused her of stealing and interrogated her in a room for more than an hour. Fermino sued for false imprisonment and negligent and intentional infliction of emotional distress.

2. Fedco demurred that workers' compensation barred the claims. The trial court sustained and the appellate court affirmed.

3. The California Supreme Court held that "the basis for the exclusivity rule in workers' compensation law is the 'presumed compensation bargain, pursuant to which the employer assumes liability for industrial and personal injury or death without regard to fault in exchange for limitations on the amount of that liability."[111] It is possible for an employer to step out of its proper role.

4. Fedco's actions constituted false imprisonment. The question was whether such behavior goes beyond the "compensation bargain" (which allows for "reasonable interrogation and detention"[112]). The court found that it did.

5. Reversed.

---

[111] Casebook p. 670.
[112] Casebook p. 672

## § 9 Automobile No-Fault Insurance

### 9.1 Hager, "No-Fault Drives Again: A Contemporary Primer"

1. 26 states have some sort of no-fault system.

2. Arguments in favor: rational and efficient compensation for victims.

3. Arguments against: weakens deterrence and corrective justice.

4. "Pure" no-fault bars all auto lawsuits.

5. "Partial" no-fault allows tort actions only above a certain threshold, either verbal (in which eligible injuries are defined) or monetary (victims can bring tort claims for damages above a certain level).

6. "Choice" no-fault allows drivers to choose either no-fault coverage or tort lawsuit rights.

7. Congressional "neo-partial" no-fault allows victims to sue if the driver was intoxicated or engaged in intentional misconduct.

8. "Cost and compensation advantages are greatest when no-fault is closest to pure."[113]

9. "Though studies are mixed, it seems unlikely that no-fault seriously undermines road safety. It is also unlikely to augment it."[114]

---

[113] Casebook p. 693.
[114] Casebook p. 694.

# § 10 Defamation

## 10.1 Defamatory Assertion of Fact

1. Common law defamation consists of defamatory assertions of fact against the plaintiff negligently or intentionally published. Under the common law, defendants who published defamatory material were held strictly liable. Now, there are constitutional requirements that the defendant act negligently or recklessly in some cases.[115]

2. The Restatement (Second) defines a defamatory statement as one that "tends so to harm the reputation of another as to lower him in the estimation of the community or to deter third persons from associating or dealing with him."[116]

3. "Only assertions of fact that can be proven false are subject to liability for defamation."[117]

4. *Libel per se*: a statement is defamatory on its face.

5. *Libel per quod*: a statement is defamatory in the context of other information (e.g., "A married B" is not defamatory unless the listener knows A is already married to C).[118]

6. Defamation must be measured by the standard of the "right-thinking person."[119]

7. *Colloquium*: if it is not obvious that the statement refers to the plaintiff, the plaintiff must prove colloquium (i.e., necessary facts).[120]

### 10.1.1 *Kaplan v. Newsweek Magazine, Inc.*

1. Kaplan sued Newsweek for libel for publishing an article criticizing his class at Stanford. The district court dismissed the claim.

2. The Ninth Circuit affirmed, holding that the statements were non-defamatory or statements of opinion rather than of fact.

### 10.1.2 *Kaelin v. Globe Communications, Inc.*

1. Kaelin sued the National Examiner over a headline that implied that the police thought he had murdered O.J. Simpson's wife and her friend.

---

[115] Casebook p. 697.
[116] Casebook p. 697.
[117] Casebook p. 702.; *Milkovich v. Lorain Journal Co.*, 497 U.S. 1 (1990).
[118] Casebook p. 705.
[119] Casebook pp. 705–06.
[120] Casebook p. 706.

2. The court held that a jury question existed. The measure is whether an "average reader" would be likely to interpret the statement as the plaintiff claimed. "So long as the publication is reasonably susceptible of a defamatory meaning, a factual question for the jury exists."[121]

### 10.1.3 Defamation in Fiction: *Bindrim v. Mitchell*

Works of fiction can be defamatory if a reasonable person would identify a character as a real person.

1. Mitchell attended Bindrim's "Nude Marathon" therapy sessions on the condition that she would not write about them. She later published a book containing similar events. Bindrim sued.

2. The jury found for Bindrim.

3. Mitchell argued that the character in the novel could not be identified as Bindrim.

4. Bindrim argued further that works of fiction cannot be defamatory. The court rejected this argument, holding that "[t]he test is whether a reasonable person, reading the book, would understand that the fictional character therein pictured was, in actual fact, the plaintiff acting as described."[122]

5. Whether the novel was defamatory was a jury question. The jury's verdict cannot be overturned. Affirmed.

## 10.2 Libel Versus Slander

1. **Slander**: spoken. Except for four categories of slander per se,[123] slander requires proof of special (i.e., pecuniary) damages as a prerequisite to recover for nonpecuniary damages (e.g., pain and suffering).

2. **Libel**: recorded. There is no requirement to prove special damages to recover for emotional distress.

### 10.2.1 Restatement (Second)

#### § 568: Libel and Slander Distinguished

1. "...no respectable authority has ever attempted to justify the distinction [between libel and slander regarding the special damages requirement] in principle..."[124] The distinction is rooted in the divide between ecclesiastical and common law courts, and "although indefensible in principle, was too well established to be repudiated."[125]

---

[121] Casebook p. 701.
[122] Casebook p. 704.
[123] See Restatement (Second) § 570 below.
[124] Casebook p. 707.
[125] Casebook p. 708.

## 10 DEFAMATION

### § 568A: Radio and Television

1. Defamatory material broadcasted or disseminated is libel.

### § 569: Liability without Proof of Special Harm—Libel

1. There is no need to prove special harm resulting from publication.

### § 570: Liability without Proof of Special Harm—Slander

1. Slander *does* require proof of special harm unless the material alleges:[126]

    (a) A criminal offense.

    (b) A loathsome disease.

    (c) Matter incompatible with his business, trade, or profession.

    (d) Serious sexual misconduct.

### § 575: Slander Creating Liability Because of Special Harm

1. Slander creates liability on the basis of special harm.

2. Special harm is the loss of something with economic or pecuniary value.

3. The special harm requirement has been expanded to include loss of companionship, etc., when the companionship has a monetary value.

4. Loss of the material advantages of hospitality can constitute special harm.

### § 623: Emotional Distress and Resulting Bodily Harm

1. One who is liable for libel or slander can also be liable for causing emotional distress.

## 10.3 Publication

### 10.3.1 Publication Requirement for Libel: *Weidman v. Ketcham*

1. A post office employee sent a postcard in an envelope to a man demanding payment for stolen apples. The man sued for libel.

2. At trial, the jury found for the plaintiff, but the court granted the defendant's motion to set aside the verdict. The appellate court reversed.

3. The defendant argued that there had been no publication and therefore there could be no liability for libel. The court held that without evidence of publication (and in this case, without evidence that the postmaster knew the identity of the recipient) there could be no liability for libel. Reversed.

---

[126]Casebook p. 710.

## 10.4 Constitutional Culpability Requirement

1. Public officials must show "*New York Times* malice."

2. Public figures must also meet the public official standard.

3. Private plaintiffs in public controversies do not need to prove *New York Times* malice, though they must prove fault ("generally understood to mean negligence toward the truth").[127]

4. The plaintiff now has the burden of proving that the defamation was false. (Under the common law, the defendant had the burden of proving truth.)[128]

### 10.4.1 Defamation of Public Officals: *New York Times Co. v. Sullivan*

There is a higher burden of proof for defamation of public officials. In addition to falsehood, the plaintiff must prove that the defendant knew the statements were false or acted recklessly towards the truth.

1. The *New York Times* ran a full page ad describing civil rights abuses of several public officials in Montgomery, Alabama. It contained several factual errors which were apparently unwitting.

2. Sullivan, a Commissioner of Mongomery, Alabama, sued for libel. The state trial court found for the plaintiff and the Alabama Supreme Court affirmed.

3. Justice Brennan:

    (a) Learned Hand: The First Amendment "presupposes that right conclusions are more likely to be gathered out of a multitude of tongues, than through any kind of authoritative selection. To many this is, and always will be, folly; but we have staked upon it our all."[129]

    (b) A rule requiring absolute factual accuracy in criticism of public officials leads to self-censorship.

    (c) Proving defamation of a public official requires "actual malice" in addition to falsehood.

    (d) Reversed.

4. "*New York Times* malice" requires that the defendant knew the statements were false or acted recklessly towards the truth. It is distinct from common law malice, which refers to hatred, ill will, or reckless disregard.[130]

---

[127] Casebook p. 727 n. 2.
[128] Casebook p. 731.
[129] Casebook p. 716.
[130] Casebook p. 719.

### 10.4.2 Defamation of Public Figures: *Gertz v. Robert Welch, Inc.*

Public figures, like public officials, must also prove *New York Times* malice to recover damages for defamation. In matters of public concern, private individuals cannot recover against publishers without proving actual malice.

1. A Chicago policeman, Nuccio, shot a youth, Nelson. Nelson's family retained an attorney, Getz, to represent them in civil litigation against Nuccio.

2. Robert Welch, Inc. was the publisher of the *American Opinion*, a magazine of the John Birch society. It published an article rife with falsehoods accusing Gertz of participating in a communist conspiracy against the police.

3. Justice Powell:

    (a) The issue is whether publishers have a constitutional privilege against liability for defamation against people who are not public figures or public officials.

    (b) States can define their own standards for protections of publishers from liability, as long as the standard requires knowledge of falsehood or reckless disregard for the truth.

    (c) Welch also argued that Gertz was a "public figure" and therefore that the *New York Times* standard should apply. The Court here held that protections could extend to public figures who "voluntarily inject" themselves into public controversies. In this case, however, Gertz was not a public figure, so he was entitled to the stricter protections afforded private citizens.

    (d) Reversed.

### 10.4.3 Defamation in Private Affairs: *Dun & Bradstreet, Inc. v. Greenmoss Builders, Inc.*

1. Dun & Bradstreet, a credit reporting agency, mistakenly misrepresented Greenmoss's assets and liabilities.

2. Greenmoss sought compensatory and punitive damages in Vermont state court. The jury returned $50,000 in compensatory damages and $300,000 in punitive damages.

3. On appeal, Dun & Bradstreet argued that plaintiffs should not be able to recover damages in defamation actions without showing actual malice.

4. Justice Powell: "permitting recovery of presumed and punitive damages in defamation cases absent a showing of 'actual malice' does not violate the First Amendment when the defamatory statements do not involve matters of public concern."

5. Affirmed.

## 10.5 Privileges

1. At common law, **absolute privilege** extends to statements in legislatures, in judicial proceedings, and by high executive officials in official capacities. Private conversations between spouses are also absolutely protected from defamation liability.

2. A **qualified privilege** exists where a speaker tries to protect the interest of the person he is speaking to—e.g., a recommender of a job applicant to the employer. The privilege is qualified because it can be negated through bad faith, recklessness, or excessive communication.

3. The **fair and accurate report** privilege allows republication of defamatory material in the context of governmental proceedings and public meetings. Whether the privilege extends to defamation beyond official proceedings is in controversy.

4. Retraction can mitigate defamation liability.

5. 47 U.S.C. § 230 grants immunity to Internet providers for republishing defamatory material from third-party providers.

### 10.5.1 Speech or Debate Clause: *Hutchinson v. Proxmire*

The Speech or Debate Clause protects members of Congress from defamation actions over statements they make in leglslatures. The privilege does not extend to statements in communications to constituents.

1. Senator Proxmire instituted the "Golden Fleece" award, criticizing examples of what he considered wasteful government spending. One of the recipients of the award, Hutchinson, was a behavioral research scientist who studied anger in animals. Proxmire announced the award in a speech published in the congressional record and in mailings to his constituents. Hutchinson sued Proxmire and his legislative assistant for libel.

2. The Speech or Debate Clause provides that members of Congress "...shall in all Cases, except Treason, Felony, and Breach of the Peace, be privileged from Arrest during their attendance at the Session of their Respective Houses, and in going to and from the same; and for any Speech or Debate in either House, they shall not be questioned in any other Place."[131]

3. Proxmire argued that the Speech or Debate Clause protects both his speech and his newsletters. He argued further that the newsletters were protected under the "informing function" of Congress.

4. Justice Burger: while the clause protects congressional speeches, "[w]e are unable to discern any 'conscious choice' to grant immunity for defamatory statements scattered far and wide by mail, press, and the electronic

---
[131] Art. I, § 6, cl. 1.

## 10 DEFAMATION

media."[132] Also, Proxmire misconstrued the meaning of "inform." The informing function refers to Congress's ability to inform itself, not for it to inform the public.

### 10.5.2 News Media Privilege: *Brown v. Kelly Broadcasting Co.*

News media do not have a "public interest" privilege.

1. Brown sued Kelly Broadcasting for defamation in a TV news report suggesting that Brown, a contractor, did shoddy work for recipients of government home improvement loans.

2. Cal. Civ. Code § 47(3) privileges communications made without malice when the speaker and recipient share a common interest. Kelly argued that § 47(3) created a "public interest" protection for news media. The court rejected this argument because it would grant protection to almost all news media communications and there was no evidence of legislative intent to create such a broad scope.

3. Mansfield: "Whenever a man publishes he publishes at his peril." Holmes: "If the publication was libellous the defendant took the risk."[133]

---

[132]Casebook p. 735.
[133]Casebook p. 740.

# § 11 Privacy

1. There are traditionally four privacy torts:

    (a) Intrusion upon seclusion.

    (b) Unauthorized use of name or likeness.

    (c) Giving unreasonable publicity to private matters.

    (d) Publicly characterizing a party in a false light.

## 11.1 Intrusion upon Seclusion

1. The intrusion must be highly offensive to a reasonable person.

2. There is no requirement of publication or communication.

### 11.1.1 *Pearson v. Dodd*

1. Members of Senator Thomas Dodd's staff surreptitiously copied documents from the Senator's office and sent them to reporters, Pearson and Anderson.

2. The distric court denied summary judgment for invasion of privacy.

3. The Fifth Circuit affirmed, holding that the intrusion constitutes the tort. Publication is not one of the elements.

4. Dissent: information obtained through these means would not be admissible as evidence in court, but we allow it for news media. "There is an anomaly lurking in this situation: the news media regard themselves as quasi-public institutions yet they deman immunity from the restraints which they vigorously demand be placed on government."[134]

### 11.1.2 *Dietemann v. Time, Inc.*

1. Employees of Time collaborated with the District Attorney's office to fraudulently gain access to Dietemann's home. Dietemann was suspect of practicing medicine without a license. They secretly recorded conversations and events. When Dietemann was arrested, the reporters took pictures, which Dietemann consented to only because he thought the police officers required it. Time published the material in an article titled "Crackdown on Quackery."

2. The district court held that the pictures taken without Dietemann's consent inside his home constituted an invasion of privacy.

3. The Ninth Circuit affirmed, holding that Dietemann had an expectation of privacy within his home. An opposite holding would chill candid speech.

---

[134] Casebook p. 746.

# 11 PRIVACY

2. Sipple sued on the argument that although his gay identity was known locally and in some community, he had not told his family, and he suffered emotional distress when they found out through the news media.

3. The trial court granted summary judgment for the Chronicle.

4. The appellate court affirmed, finding that the facts were newsworthy and already well known publicly to many.

## 11.4 False Light

1. "False light is established where the defendant publicizes false, objectionable information about the plaintiff." The publicity must be highly offensive to a reasonable person and there must be proof of *New York Times* malice.[137]

2. False light is distinct from defamation in a few ways:

    (a) False light requires **publicity** (communication to the general public), while defamation only requires *publication* (communication to one person other than the victim).

    (b) **Both private and public figures** must prove *New York Times* malice.

    (c) Defamation requires harm to the victim's reputation. False light only requires **offensiveness**.

### 11.4.1 Distinguishing Common Law and *New York Times* Malice: *Cantrell v. Forest City Publ'g Co.*

Plaintiffs claiming false light must prove *New York Times* malice but not common law malice.

1. Margaret Cantrell's husband was killed in a bridge collapse. Some months later, the Plain Dealer newspaper published a piece on the Cantrell family's poverty after the disaster, which included a number of falsehoods.

2. In *Time, Inc. v. Hill*, the Court held that newsworthy people have a right to recovery when material and substantial falsification occurred.[138]

3. In *New York Times v. Sullivan*, the Court held that public officials can recover with proof that the defendant published the false claim "with knowledge of its falsity or in reckless disregard of the truth" (i.e., "actual malice").[139]

---

[137] Casebook p. 769.
[138] Casebook p. 767.
[139] Casebook p. 767.

## 11 PRIVACY

4. On the free speech question: "The First Amendment is not a license to trespass, to steal, or to intrude by electronic means into the precincts of another's home or office. It does not become such a license simply because the person subjected to the intrusion is reasonably suspected of committing a crime."[135]

## 11.2 Appropriation of Name or Likeness

1. Defendants are liable for unauthorized appropriation of the name or likeness for their own use.

2. There is a fuzzy line between tortious appropriation and legitimate use.

3. Aspects of identity beyond name and likeness can be included (e.g., *Here's Johnny Portable Toilets*[136]).

4. Celebrities can also sue under a right to publicity tort (e.g., *Sagan v. Apple Computer*).

### 11.2.1 Newsworthiness: *Neff v. Time, Inc.*

A photograph taken in public with consent can be published if it is newsworthy.

1. A Sports Illustrated photographer took a picture of Neff, with consent, at a Steelers game with his fly down. The magazine used it in a feature on Steelers fans with the caption "a strange kind of love."

2. Neff sued for (1) appropriation of name or likeness and (2) publicity given to private life.

3. The court held for the defendant because the photo was "newsworthy."

## 11.3 Publicity of Private Life

1. **Publicizing private details** is tortious if it would be highly offensive to a reasonable person and is not of legitimate concern to the public. The facts must actually be private (see *Sipple* below).

### 11.3.1 No Cause of Action if Material is Already Public: *Sipple v. Chronicle Publ'g Co.*

A plaintiff has no action for being outed as gay in a newspaper if he is already out in public in other contexts.

1. Sipple prevented Sara Jane Moore from shooting President Ford. The San Francisco Chronicle published a piece on Sipple mentioning his role in the gay community.

---

[135] Casebook p. 752.
[136] Casebook p. 758.

4. The trial court struck Cantrell's demand for punitive damages, finding that the defendant had not acted with malice. The appellate court interpreted this finding to mean that there was no *New York Times* malice and therefore that the trial court should have directed a verdict for the defendants.

5. The Supreme Court held that the appellate court confused common law malice with *New York Times* malice. It held that there was sufficient evidence for a jury to find the defendant acted with *New York Times* malice, even if it lacked common law malice.

## 11.5 IIED and Public Figures: *Hustler Magazine v. Falwell*

To claim intentional infliction of emotional distress from published material, public figures and officials must also show *New York Times* malice.

1. *Hustler* published parody of a Campari ad campaign featuring Jerry Falwell with the caption "Jerry Falwell talks about his first time" and other jabs. The ad included a disclaimer: "ad parody—not to be taken seriously."

2. "...public figures as well as public officials will be subject to 'vehement, caustic, and sometimes unpleasantly sharp attacks."[140]

3. Falwell and the appellate court take the view that if an outrageous utterance intended to cause emotional distress did in fact cause distress, "it is of no constitutional import whether the statement was a fact or an opinion, or whether it was true or false."[141]

4. The Supreme Court, Justice Rehnquist: "We conclude that public figures and public officials may not recover for the tort of intentional infliction of emotional distress by reason of publications such as the one here at issue without showing in addition that the publication contains a false statement of fact which was made with 'actual malice,' i.e., with the knowledge that the statement was false or with reckless disregard as to whether or not it was true."[142]

---

[140] Casebook p. 57.
[141] Casebook p. 58.
[142] Casebook p. 60.

www.ingramcontent.com/pod-product-compliance
Lightning Source LLC
Chambersburg PA
CBHW062224220526
45471CB00009B/3335